LOVE, SEX, AND STAYING WARM

CREATING A VITAL RELATIONSHIP

LOVE, SEX, AND STAYING WARM

CREATING A VITAL RELATIONSHIP

Neil Rosenthal

Flagstaff Mountain Press
Boulder, Colorado

Revised Edition January 2016

ISBN
978-0-9969858-0-2 (Paperback)
978-0-9969858-1-9 (eBook/.ePub)
978-0-9969858-2-6 (eBook/Kindle)

Flagstaff Mountain Press
Boulder, Colorado
www.heartrelationships.com

To Roni, Dreamer and Indy.
I belong to you.

CONTENTS

Love, Sex, and Staying Warm

FOREWORD

Neil Rosenthal's connection with the Denver Post goes back many years, but I wasn't introduced to him until 2012, when I asked him to not only begin sharing his relationship column with us again, but something much more personal.

Wildfires were raging across the Front Range of Colorado, and hundreds of people were losing their homes, pets, and livelihoods.

This was something with which Neil had experience. In 2010 he and his now-wife Roni were on their way back home from a morning hike with their dogs in Boulder's Fourmile Canyon when they smelled smoke. Neil could hear airplanes and helicopters nearby so he thought everything was under control.

"I figured wrong. There were no planes or helicopters," he recalled. "I had been hearing the roar of an approaching forest fire raging toward us." The couple and their pets narrowly escaped in their car. Eight days passed before they could return, only to find everything burned beyond recognition. They eventually learned that the fire had come through the trail they were on and had they started their hike any later, they would have died.

In 2012, a different area of Colorado, including Boulder was hit by wildfire, with a greater loss of property. This time, Neil and

Roni's home was spared, but it brought back memories. Because Neil is so accomplished in his daily practice and columns with helping people pick up the pieces when their love lives and personal affairs fall apart, I asked him if he could help guide people to healing after they lose all their personal possessions in a violent, devastating fire.

He agreed, and the resulting five-part series had good advice that people still comment about how helpful it was and what fans they are of Neil's to me three years later.

We're taught from a young age that people and lives matter, and that we shouldn't mourn the loss of favorite objects. But it hurts to lose things. Neil told people whose homes had burned to the ground that it was OK to feel sad and angry that they no longer had precious photographs, mementos from their loved ones, and something as basic as the clothing in their closet. He gave them coping mechanisms and practical advice for how to move on.

Not only did he offer folks a way to climb out of their despair, he later conducted free workshops for communities affected by the fire that we helped publicize.

Ever since then, Neil has been back to writing his relationship advice column, offering people guidance as they go through courtship, marriage, divorce, death, and dealing with all kinds of problems.

Heaven forbid that we'd skip a week of sharing his advice. I won't soon forget the angry calls I got from readers when he had to hold his column once because a lengthy story took up space we usually devoted to him in the features section.

What I--and his readers--love about Neil is his openness, his honesty, and his encouragement to men and women that it's OK to have feelings and express them—in fact it's mandatory if you want warm and loving relationships.

I love that he instructs readers to be a "student" husband or wife—that you need the attitude of a beginner to learn to understand, listen to, and appreciate your lover. He's also not afraid to emphasize how important physical contact is in a relationship and how to rekindle the flame that invariably dies down.

Readers value having someone real they can send their deeply personal questions to, and Neil always responds honestly, often pointing out things they might not have recognized or addressed in their relationships with friends and lovers.

My interest in his work is selfish as well. I've been happily married for thirty-plus years and welcome reminders from Neil about how to keep my own relationship vital and interesting.

He's sure to improve yours as well.

Suzanne S. Brown,
Senior Editor, Features
The Denver Post

ACKNOWLEDGMENTS

To my navigator at Redbrush, Phil Whitmarsh, whose patient encouragement, assistance, and recommendations I found invaluable in rethinking this edition of the book. And to Burke Allen, my publicist at Allen Media Strategies. I am indebted to both of these gentlemen for helping to make my dream of this second edition come true.

Neil Rosenthal

NOTES FROM THE AUTHOR

After spending thirty-five years as a marriage/relationship counselor, and having written a weekly syndicated newspaper column read by millions of people through the years in the United States, Canada, New Zealand, and Australia (and also the Philippines, Kenya, South Africa, Great Britain, India, France and so on—where I'm not published in newspapers but am still widely read)—I have finally decided to compile a guide of some of my best writings that will help most every couple—married or not—to improve their relationship.

This is not designed as a textbook. You can open this book to virtually any page and find a valuable relationship skill that will assist you almost immediately. Therefore, this book was not compiled for you to read cover to cover, and I have not put these chapters in order on purpose. It was designed for you to page through and land on a subject or a chapter that interests you or that you're seeking assistance with, and therefore for you to skip around the book at will.

A couple can thus read this book together or separately. The book can stay on the nightstand to be used for a bedtime exercise, or in the living/family room as a guide about how to deepen the connection, closeness, and intimacy between the two of you.

Most every chapter speaks about the skills necessary in order to create and sustain a vital relationship. You can examine what emotions are necessary to invest in a relationship , or how to more effectively communicate with each other.

If anger or the inability to effectively resolve conflicts or disagreements is troubling your relationship—or if you have a difficult time communicating more effectively when you're hurt or angry, then you will be particularly interested in the chapter on A Couple's Exercise to Effectively Resolve Conflict that addresses the subjects of how to control anger, of how to handle criticism better, of how to be less defensive, how to break a power struggle, or how to resolve conflicts, issues or disagreements.

The most noteworthy chapters of the book are dedicated to keeping your relationship close and intimate, and how to avoid losing the closeness, the connection and the intimacy between the two of you.

There are also a variety of chapters on romance, seduction tips, sexual "secrets," and wooing—including how to jump-start your sex life if it has recently been comatose.

There are also chapters regarding forgiveness, romantic intelligence, and what sabotages a relationship. In addition, you will find chapters on hidden issues your relationship may be tripping over, cell phone addiction, relationship deal-breakers, how to stop being possessive and jealous, deepening a relationship, quizzes on evaluating your relationship, as well as chapters regarding how worthy of love you feel and how you might feel better about yourself.

Finally, there's a discussion about keeping your relationship intact when you're going through a crisis, money arguments, a chapter on the differences between the marriage in the eyes of the church, the state (your marriage certificate) and the psychological marriage, the secrets of compatibility and a couple of chapters on trust or rebuilding trust.

This book is designed for both newlyweds and couples married forty-five-plus years: for people who are dating, living together, or struggling with issues, differences, or conflicts; for couples who are deeply in love and for couples who have fallen out of love; for people attempting to recover from a breach of trust; for couples who would just like to add greater levels of connection, romance, and affection to their relationship—and for couples who want more sex—or better sex.

I hope you enjoy it.

Neil Rosenthal
Boulder, Colorado

Neil Rosenthal

QUIZ: WHAT GRADE WOULD YOU GET IN YOUR RELATIONSHIP?

If you were to give yourself a grade for how effective, how responsive and how loving you behave in your relationship, what would that grade be?

Better yet, break the above question down into smaller segments. On an A B C D F scale, using (+) or (—) to more fully adjust your grade, what grade would you give yourself in the following categories?

___ How affectionate are you?

___ How romantic?

___ How sexy (or sexually responsive) are you?

___ How generous?

___ How trusting?

___ How kind are you?

___ How much fun are you to be around?

___ How emotionally present are you?

___ How physically present are you?

___ How sensitive and compassionate are you to your mate's feelings?

___ How good a listener are you with your partner?

___ How emotionally nurturing are you?

___ How physically nurturing?

___ How financially nurturing?

___ How much of a friend are you to your intimate partner?

___ How much in control are you of your negative emotions (such as anger, volatility, insecurity, jealousy, anxiety, fear, and mistrust)?

___ Showing your mate how much you value him/her?

___ How affectionate and physically tender are you (without ulterior motives)?

___ How responsive and accommodating are you to what your partner says s/he wants or needs?

___ How financially responsible and accountable are you?

___ How respectful are you of your partner?

___ Overall, how much effort do you give to your relationship?

___ Your level of commitment.

___ Your receptivity to different ways of doing thing flexibility in changing your routines or trying some

___ Your willingness to address difficult issues or deal with conflicts proactively.

___ Your ability to engage in a disagreement effectively and skillfully.

___ Your overall attitude about the relationship or around your partner.

___ Your sense of humor.

___ The division of chores, roles, responsibilities, duties.

___ Behaving, thinking, and planning as a couple rather than as two individuals.

___ The time, attention, effort, skill, and patience you bring to parenting.

___ Teamwork: how you operate as a team player in the relationship.

___ Your ability and willingness to make up after a fight or a disagreement.

Most of us have this notion that we're going to find the right person to be with and then we'll be deliriously happy, content, and fulfilled. Seldom do we think about being the right person—making ourself the best intimate partner we can possibly be—more romantic, more loving, more giving, more communicative, more compassionate, and more in charge of our negative emotions and reactions.

What might you gain if you committed yourself to improving some of these grades? If that interests you, explore the following questions carefully:

- If you were going to improve some of your grades, what would you have to do differently?
- What would you have to quit doing?
- When would you be willing to begin?
- How might you keep yourself motivated when the going gets rough?
- What could you say to your partner when you fall down on the job or when you need help?

"As a general thing, people marry most happily with their own kind. The trouble lies in the fact that people usually marry at an age when they do not really know what their own kind is." (Robertson Davies)

HOW WORTHY OF LOVE ARE YOU?

A woman falls in love with a man. She is wild about him and will follow him anywhere. But he has a hard time believing that she loves him and interprets her love as neediness or loneliness. However, she is so smitten by him that she simply won't let him go. He finally accepts that she genuinely desires and wants him but then begins to wonder what is wrong with her. He judges and criticizes what he thinks is wrong with her so often that she finally leaves him. When she is gone, he says to himself: "I knew she didn't really love me."

A woman who describes herself as "a mess" meets a man who thinks she is the woman of his dreams. After a short courtship, he proposes. But nothing he does can remove the feeling she holds that she is unworthy of his love and devotion, so she takes on a project at work that requires her to work extra-long hours. The man waits this out for a while but becomes increasingly angry at her and eventually gives up and leaves. She goes out and meets another man, and the pattern repeats itself.

A man and a woman marry, and they are happily in love. But before long he grows bored with the routine and the sameness, so he runs into another woman's arms. His wife finds out and asks him if he wants a divorce. He says yes, explaining that maybe he isn't meant to be married.

These vignettes speak of a pattern of behaviors that define one aspect of failed romance: I am unlikely to attain romantic happiness if I don't feel worthy of love, and I therefore push away from or sabotage love when it is offered to me.

If I feel worthy of love, I will feel worthy of being loved by you. I will feel worthy of your respect, your friendship, your devotion, and your commitment. In addition, I am likely to feel self-love, self-respect, and self-acceptance. I will feel competent in meeting the essential challenges life throws at me and empowered in my dealings with the world.

If I don't feel worthy of love, I won't feel as if I measure up or that I'm good enough, and therefore I'm far more likely to not allow myself to love at all. If I don't feel I measure up, I'm going to have a hard time trusting you when you say you love me, because I "know" that I'm not worthy of love, and therefore I assume that when you really get to know me, you won't want me anymore and will eventually dump me.

So, either I choose someone who is likely to reject me, or I give myself an excuse in order to reject, abandon, or betray you—or I force you to reject me. In essence, I will reject you before you can reject me.

So permit me to ask you, on a scale from 0—10, how worthy of love do you feel? If your answer is lower than you want it to be, here are a few things you can do:

- Make as large a list as you can about what you like or respect about yourself. What inner resources do you use to get through a trauma or a challenging time? With whom have

you behaved with compassion or kindness? When
been courageous? How are you creative? In which si
have you demonstrated great social skills? How do you take good care of yourself and of others? What do you like about your appearance? When have you been a good friend? A good sibling? A good child to your parents? A good parent to your children? What do you offer a mate in a romantic relationship? Refer to this list often. It will remind you about why you may be more lovable than you think.

- Act with integrity and honor in your dealings with the world.
- Quit doing things that will hurt you or other people.
- Take overall better care of yourself.
- Accept responsibility for where you are in life right now, and decide if you want to make any changes in the direction your life is going.
- Clean up all negative relationships and unfinished emotional business you have with others.
- Let hope run your life rather than fear.

Groucho: So, Mrs. Smith. Do you have any children?

Mrs. Smith: Yes, thirteen.

Groucho: Thirteen! Good lord, isn't that a burden?

Mrs. Smith: Well, I love my husband.

Groucho: Lady, I love my cigar, but I take it out of my mouth once in a while. (Groucho Marx and a contestant on the game show *You Bet Your Life*.)

QUIZ: HOW COMFORTABLE ARE YOU IN RECEIVING LOVE?

Below are questions designed to help you discover how comfortable you are in receiving love. Rank each item with S for "sometimes" O for "often," R for "rarely," or N for "never."

___ Do you feel uncomfortable when somebody brags about you?

___ Do you feel negative toward someone else who is bragged about?

___ Do you get gifts and then feel obligated?

___ Do you devalue the gifts others give you?

___ Do you deflect compliments when you get them?

___ Do you ask for something, get it, and then find something wrong with it?

___ Do you find yourself mainly remembering only the "bad times"?

___ Does it seem to you that no one wants you to have what you want?

___ Do you say "I want you to offer it," and when your partner does, you say your partner offered it only because you asked for it?

___ Do you feel uncomfortable when another person is getting all the attention?

___ Do you feel like "nothing is ever good enough"?

___ Do you feel uncomfortable wanting things for yourself?

___ Do you say you don't want it then complain about not getting it?

___ Do you see everyone else as having what they want?

___ Do you have trouble accepting other's positive evaluations of your worth and your ability?

___ Do you feel uncomfortable giving something to yourself?

___ Do you feel critical of someone who is needy?

___ Do you feel like a bad person?

___ Do you feel worthless?

___ Do you feel like a failure?

___ Do you feel depressed?

___ Do you feel anger at others who are fortunate?

___ Do you have trouble imaging how others can accept praise?

___ Do you feel uncomfortable with people who want nurturing?

___ Do you feel like you have nothing to give?

___ Do you get a compliment and think "If you knew what I was really like, you would not say that"?

___ Do you feel uncomfortable asking for nurturing?

___ Do you get what you ask for, but then feel empty?

To calculate your comfort in receiving love, count the items marked R and multiply by 2.Then count the total items marked S and O and multiply by 2. If your R number is greater than your S+O number, it means your ability to receive love is greater than your impulse to push it away. If your S+O number is higher than your R number, then you have a more difficult time receiving and accepting love. If that's the case, this quiz assists you in knowing which opportunities are available to you in order for you take in more love than you currently do.

Ask your partner to take the assessment also, and then dialogue with each other about your discoveries.

Source: *Receiving Love* by Harville Hendrix and Helen LaKelly Hunt (Atria Publishers).

"When two people are under the influence of the most violent, most insane, most delusive and most transient of passions, they are required to swear that they will remain in that excited, abnormal and exhausting condition until death do them part."
(George Bernard Shaw)

DISCOVERING THE LINK TO YOUR HIDDEN ISSUES

When you are squabbling with your intimate partner over petty, small, nitpicky things, could you describe with confidence the hidden, more subterranean issues that you are fighting about?

Most people can't. Most people have, at best, an extremely vague idea about what pushes their buttons, or why they get so triggered about certain behaviors. They may know they're in a power struggle with their spouse or intimate partner, but they have poor understanding what they're actually fighting for.

Why are you so sensitive to accusations, words, or behaviors from your partner? Exactly why do some things make you fighting mad? Where are your buttons? Why are they there, and what can you do to gain better insight and mastery over them?

If you want answers to those questions, write as many responses as you can to the following questions: "When I was a child, what did I want from my mother that I did not get? What did I want from my father that I did not get?" Create at least half a dozen answers for each of your parents.

Your answers will likely point to the issues that mean the most to you in your adult life. And you can be sure those are the issues that will emerge and what you will fight for in your intimate relationship.

For example, let's say you grew up wanting more approval from your father. As an adult, it is very likely that you will need and want your intimate partner's consistent approval, and that you will be very reactive and/or defensive about receiving his/ her disapproval. So if your mate becomes judgmental or critical of you, you can expect that you will get defensive, angry or argue more with him/her. You will be fighting for acceptance, acknowledgment and approval, and will be particularly sensitive to your mate's disapproval, judgment or criticism.

Another example: Let's say your mother was controlling and manipulative, and used guilt to keep you in line. Now you're in an adult relationship, but you're still sensitive to anyone—especially an intimate partner—attempting to control, manipulate, guilt or play martyr toward you. That touches such a raw nerve, you respond with greater anger and reactivity than the situation would normally call for. But because of your past, this issue is extremely sensitive to you, and you remain hyper-vigilant in order to defend yourself from anyone being manipulative or controlling.

Take the lists you created from the questions above and look them over carefully. These are your hidden issues, the deeper, subterranean sensitivities you have that no doubt come out over and over again in your intimate relationships with others.

It is our work to make peace with our inner sensitivities and to reduce the hold they have over us. If we don't do that work, we will wind up charging our intimate partners a steep price. Perhaps we'll be more suspicious, less trusting, more on guard and held back, or quicker to hurt or anger—all of which, over time, could have a huge impact on the quality of your relationship.

These are the issues that you must be alert to, because they will come out with more force and power than other issues. You may always be sensitive to someone who manipulates, controls or guilt trips you—to use our examples from above. But it becomes your work to reduce the power these hidden issues have over you. They come from your childhood, they're your unmet or inadequately met childhood needs, and they're your trigger buttons.

To discuss these sensitivities with your spouse would be extremely valuable. It just might save your relationship.

"By all means marry: If you get a good wife, you'll become happy; if you get a bad one, you'll become a philosopher." (Socrates)

WHAT WOMEN REALLY WANT

Young King Arthur was ambushed and imprisoned by the monarch of a neighboring kingdom. The monarch could have killed him but was moved by Arthur's youth and ideals. So, the monarch offered him his freedom, as long as he could answer a very difficult question. Arthur would have a year to figure out the answer and, if after a year, he still had no answer, he would be put to death.

The question? What do women really want?

Such a question would perplex even the most knowledgeable man, and to young Arthur, it seemed an impossible query. But, since it was better than death, he accepted the monarch's proposition to have an answer by year's end.

He returned to his kingdom and began to poll everyone: the princess, the priests, the wise men, and even the court jester. He spoke with everyone, but no one could give him a satisfactory answer.

Many people advised him to consult the old witch, because she would have the answer.

But the price would be high, as the witch was famous throughout the kingdom for the exorbitant prices she charged.

The last day of the year arrived and Arthur had no choice but to talk to the witch. She agreed to answer the question, but he would have to agree to her price first.

The old witch wanted to marry Sir Lancelot, the most noble of the Knights of the Round Table and Arthur's closest friend!

Young Arthur was horrified. She was hunchbacked and hideous, had only one tooth, smelled like sewage, and made obscene noises. He had never encountered such a repugnant creature in all his life.

He refused to force his friend to marry her and endure such a terrible burden, but Lancelot, learning of the proposal, spoke with Arthur. He said nothing was too big of a sacrifice compared to Arthur's life and the preservation of the Round Table.

Hence, a wedding was proclaimed and the witch answered Arthur's question thus:

"What a woman really wants," she answered, "is to be in charge of her own life."

Everyone in the kingdom instantly knew that the witch had uttered a great truth and that Arthur's life would be spared.

And so it was, the neighboring monarch granted Arthur his freedom—and Lancelot and the witch had a wonderful wedding.

The honeymoon hour approached and Lancelot, steeling himself for a horrific experience, entered the bedroom. But, what a sight awaited him. The most beautiful woman he had ever seen lay before him on the bed. The astounded Lancelot asked what had happened.

The beauty replied that since he had been so kind to her when she appeared as a witch, she would henceforth, be her horrible deformed self only half the time and the beautiful maiden the other half.

Which would he prefer? Beautiful during the day or night? Lancelot pondered the predicament. During the day, a beautiful woman to show off to his friends. But at night, in the privacy of his castle, an old witch? Or, would he prefer having a hideous witch during the day, but by night, a beautiful woman for him to enjoy wondrous intimate moments?

What would YOU do?

What Lancelot chose is below.

BUT make YOUR choice before you peak down below. OKAY?

Noble Lancelot said that he would allow HER to make the choice herself.

Upon hearing this, she announced that she would be beautiful all the time because he had respected her enough to let her be in charge of her own life.

What is the moral to this story? The moral is...

If you don't let a woman have her own way, things are going to get ugly.

—Anonymous

"Some day after we have mastered the winds, the waves, the tides and gravity, we shall harness for God the energies of love. And then, for the second time in the history of the world, man will have discovered fire." (Taillard de Chardin)

CHANCE ENCOUNTERS

Imagine the following: You are running late to meet a friend for lunch. Because you are in a hurry, you find yourself speeding down an icy road. A police car spots you, pulls you over and tickets you for speeding. You curse your bad luck. When the police officer finally lets you go, you pass by a major car wreck—just blocks from where you were stopped. You pull over to lend assistance and discover that the driver is hurt. She got in an icy skid and slammed into a telephone pole a minute or two before you drove by. You help her out of her car, call for help, take your jacket off, and wrap it around her because she is cold. You also call your lunch date and reschedule your luncheon.

How probable would it be that you and the driver—who you stay with until help arrives—might become close friends? What would you guess the chances would be that it could have been you that slammed into that telephone pole if the police officer hadn't pulled you over? If you were the hurt driver, would you feel affection or gratitude for the person who rescued you?

Throughout most days of our life, we have chance encounters with people or situations that can be—and often are—life transforming. Think back for a moment. How did you meet your spouse/sweetheart/lover? Although there are the personals or online matchmaking sites, most people meet the person of their dreams through a chance encounter—at a grocery store, or a dance class, while waiting for your car to be fixed, or in a doctor's waiting room.

How did you meet the person you view as your closest friend? Your first girlfriend/boyfriend? Your first love? When has an author unexpectedly influenced you? How about someone who has had a significant impact on the profession or job you've chosen? When has a movie you saw, a book you read, a speaker you heard or a teacher you once had changed your life?

In every chance encounter, we have the option of being open and receptive to strangers we come into contact with—or we can be largely unavailable, wrapped up in the preoccupations of our ongoing personal sagas.

But it pays off very handsomely to be open and receptive to the people we come into contact with. I remember meeting a fellow in a spontaneous classroom exercise my freshman year of college who has become a very close lifelong friend. Another time I worked with a professor/therapist who would wind up profoundly influencing my life's work and my choice of profession. I once met a woman attending a party (which I almost didn't go to) who would turn out to catch my eye, even through that relationship didn't last. And I met the woman of my dreams in a restaurant that I was hesitant to go to.

If you think about it, your life is sprinkled with such transformational chance encounters that you never would have imagined. So my advice: Stay open to the people you meet on those seemingly random encounters when fate throws the two of you together. Think for a moment: When has someone lent you a helping hand when you were in need, like the driver described above? When were you in the right place at the right time for a total stranger? How many people do you think you come into contact with on a daily/weekly/monthly basis that would be receptive to having a new friend—or would maybe be receptive to falling in love?

A chance encounter is the ultimate serendipity, an accident of happy coincidence or good fortune that transpires unexpectedly. Such encounters do not occur every day, but they do happen. And yes, they have the capacity to completely transform or alter your life.

Make sure you feel safe and are in no danger, but after that be open to the next time that life unexpectedly throws you together with someone unknown.

You never know.

"When authorities warn you of the sinfulness of sex, there is an important lesson to be learned. Do not have sex with the authorities." (Matt Groening)

HANDLING CRITICISM BETTER

What's the worst thing anyone could say about you? Of the myriad of potential answers you might come up with, let's say that your spouse or lover says that you're insecure. Instead of getting angry or defensive, let's say you were open to exploring whether the criticism was true ("Well, aren't I sometimes insecure? OK, so she just told you something true about you. Isn't that what you want from your relationship—that she tell you the truth?")

Of course, you could always go to your familiar response: "No I'm not. It's you who are insecure!"—but you know where that leads.

Once you understand that you can actually hear something critical and even gain value from it, give yourself a gift of the following exercise, compliments of Byron Katie in the book *I Need Your Love—Is That True?* (Three Rivers Press) (or www.thework.com):

Step 1. When someone criticizes you and says you are wrong (unkind, insensitive, uncaring, etc.) settle into it. Ask yourself "Is it true? Could he be right? Can I see how someone might see me that way?" Be patient and wait for the answer. Respond to the other person only with "Thank you for letting me know that."

Step 2. After the criticism, ask yourself, "Was hearing that remark at all stressful?" (If the answer is yes, it means that the criticism is very likely true about you.)

Question yourself before you permit yourself to get on the defensive. If a friend says "You don't listen to me," and you want to respond "you're wrong," do an honest exploration with yourself before you react or respond. "She's wrong about me—is that true?" Well, not exactly. The truth is that sometimes I don't listen. "How do I react when I believe that she is wrong?" I immediately get upset and feel unjustly accused. I start defending myself. I attack her in my mind. I feel sorry for myself. I stop listening.

If I were to ask myself who would I be without thinking: "She's wrong about me," what effect would that have on me? (Well, I might listen. I might be open to what she's saying. I might take a deeper look at myself.)

Now turn the statement around: "I'm wrong about her." Or "I'm wrong about me." Or "She's right about me." Are these statements as true as or truer than the original statement?

If you'd like to follow these steps with other issues in your life, here are Katie's steps which she calls "The Work." Put an issue, a problem, or a conflict into a statement (example: "He/she doesn't love me," or "I would be happier if I got that promotion.") and follow these steps.

1.) Is it true?

2.) Can you absolutely know that it's true? Can you absolutely know that you would be happier, or that your life would be better, if you got what you wanted? Can you really know what is best in the long run for his/her/your path?

3.) How do you react when you believe that thought? Where do you feel it in your body? How do you treat yourself? How do you treat others when you believe that thought? Does that thought bring peace or stress into your life? 4.) Close your eyes and imagine yourself with the person (or in that situation) without that thought. Describe how it would feel to not have that thought. How would your life be different? 5.) Turn the thought around. Find three examples in your life where the turnarounds are as true or truer.

Now take an issue in your life, a thought you have that causes you anger or defensiveness, and use these questions to explore that issue. Your need for approval will likely diminish if you do, and you are far more likely to feel greater peace of mind.

"Have you heard of this new book entitled *1001 Sex Secrets Every Men Should Know?* It contains comments from 1001 women on how men can be better in bed. I think that women would actually settle for three: Slow down, turn off the TV, call out the right name."
(Jay Leno)

HOW DO YOU DISCONNECT?

We all know that it feels more intimate to be connected to the person (or people) we care about and love. Much less understood is how a couple who starts out with lots of love and hope lose their close connection and begin the painful process of falling out of love and feeling disconnected from one another.

In order to figure out how the process of disconnection has worked in your life, let me invite you to explore the various ways you disconnect. Look at the following list of disconnecting behaviors, taken from Pat Love's book *The Truth about Love* (Fireside)—and circle the ones you use:

overworking criticizing interrupting nagging withdrawing drinking judging being irritable being distracted clinging being resentful threatening keeping secrets being rigid withholding your opinion taking on too much responsibility over functioning being pre-occupied with your own thoughts being uncooperative believing you have the right answer being a pleaser being undependable being dishonest going silent condemning forgetting embarrassing lying fault finding being perfectionistic shutting down over-spending lecturing being cynical avoiding being depressed using sarcasm bossing being rude shaming assuming coercing being impatient being tense being angry acting uncaring yelling raging pushing being perpetually late being authoritative turning away controlling withholding affection staying preoccupied not supporting interrupting withholding sex expressing hostility being aggressive showing suspicion procrastinating always wanting more looking for problems.

Now go back through this list and circle the ways your partner disconnects.

There are several reasons why people who once felt very close to each other lose their connection and grow more distant and mechanical with each other, says Love. Some of those reasons are:

- If I let myself get close to you, I fear that I will lose me, and therefore forfeit my individuality and freedom.
- The fear that you'll leave me—and that will destroy me.
- We don't spend enough time together, and we have to spend a certain amount of time together to keep the connection strong. (Quick solution: Ask yourself "What would make me want to spend more time with my partner? Or what would make my partner want to spend more time with me?")
- We're not consistently tuned into our partners, or our partner's needs or wants. Truly paying attention, taking an interest, showing you care. Being empathetic and compassionate—by walking in your partner's shoes a lot more often.

- We're not letting ourselves get too intimate, too close, too emotionally exposed. We're not revealing our inner selves to each other. The real me—vulnerabilities and all. The real you.
- The fear that I'll get what I want and I won't feel worthy of it, or that I won't be able to handle getting what I want, and therefore I'll sabotage it.

The most effective way to reconnect is to take charge of your own behaviors. Think about the partner you want to be—and the relationship you want to have—and then make a conscious choice to act in accordance with those goals.

"It requires infinitely greater genius to make love than to make war." (Nin De Lenclos)

QUIZ: EVALUATING YOUR RELATIONSHIP

This inventory offers you an opportunity to be more objective in looking at a current or previous relationship. It is not a scientifically validated questionnaire, but a guide based on my observations about what's important in a relationship—and about what gets intimate relationships in trouble.

If you are doing this as a couple, score this questionnaire individually, and do not talk about your answers or responses until both of you have completed the inventory. A discussion of how you rated things and why could be very enlightening.

5=extremely satisfied, 4=satisfied, 3=neutral, 2=dissatisfied, 1=extremely dissatisfied

1. We confide our personal feelings to each other.
2. We have similar interests and activities.
3. We respect each other.
4. We're attracted to and pleased by each other's appearance.

5. We are understanding of each other.
6. We are romantic and nurturing of each other.
7. We express affection for each other.
8. He/she is compassionate and empathetic toward me.
9. I am satisfied with how we spend money and what we spend it on.
10. We are both monogamous.
11. We are sexually compatible and comfortable with each other.
12. We like each other.
13. We have similar attitudes about having children.
14. We are complementary in the way we raise our children.
15. We communicate well.
16. We have compatible moral, religious, or spiritual practices/beliefs.
17. We agree on our social life.
18. We agree on how the house is kept.
19. I have influence over the decisions we make.
20. I am satisfied with the division of roles we have worked out.
21. We are able to talk about what is troubling our relationship when tension starts to build between us.
22. We give compliments and do favors for each other.

23. We both feel the other does his/her fair share.

24. We are compatible about our in-laws and respective families.

25. We agree on the amount of time spent together.

26. We play and have fun together.

27. I am generally happy with our relationship.

28. I am generally comfortable with the way anger is expressed in our relationship.

29. I am generally comfortable with the way conflicts and disagreements are handled.

30. I love him/her.

31. I feel loved by him/her.

32. I am generally happy with the friends we have in common and how much time we spend socially together.

33. I look forward to seeing him/her.

34. I feel valued in a serious conversation with my mate.

35. When we're together, I rarely feel lonely.

Scoring: Add up your points based on the scale at the top of the list.

141–175: Your relationship is positive and is going well. You are responsive to each other, and you usually like being around him/her.
106–140: There are problems that have developed in your relationship. Don't delay working through these things.

105 or below: Your relationship is not that happy, and it could be in jeopardy. Do something about this right away.

All questions are not equal. If you gave an intimate partner all positive scores, except that you don't like him/her or that you aren't attracted to him/her, a high score still does *not* mean things are fine.

"One of my theories is that men love with their eyes; women love with their ears." (Zsa Zsa Gabor)

HOW IMPORTANT AM I TO YOU? YOU HAVE TO SHOW ME

Dear Neil: I've been married for thirty-seven years. My husband no longer notices me. For Christmas, he bought me a book I'd already read, the same calendar I'd already purchased, and a lovely pair of earrings. I had told him about the book and calendar when I read and bought them. Last evening, I put on a nice nightgown and perfume—and he didn't even say anything—we just had sex.

I've given up trying to reach him, and I don't know how much more I can take. I've asked him to give me one compliment a week, as I don't think that's too much to ask. But recently he said he thinks I'm being selfish for asking for that. An example is: "I wish you'd tell me I look nice" and the response is: "You know you look nice so why should I say anything?" I feel invisible, and am concerned that my marriage is over. Could you address this issue?

—Invisible in Denver

Dear Neil: I've been seeing this man for over seven months. In some ways he makes me feel cherished, but in other ways it feels like he does many little things to prevent a successful reciprocal relationship.

He's very passive. I feel like I'm the only one managing to keep the relationship going much of the time. He acts very ambivalent, and I don't feel he makes an effort to show me I'm valued.

—Confused in New Orleans

Dear Invisible and Confused: One of the most common power struggles couples fight about is related to the theme in your two letters. It's the question: "How important am I to you?"

If I'm important to you, I need for you to show it—through words, being "sweet," being affectionate, romancing me, treating me as if I am valued and cherished, and being responsive to what I say is important to me. If you will show me how much I matter to you, I will feel blessed to have found you, and I will richly reciprocate as long as I am still invested in our relationship.

But if you ignore my requests, are insensitive to my needs or wishes, if you act like it isn't necessary to romance me, if you hold back affection or sweetness, if you wait for me to put forth all the effort, than I will feel unwanted, unnurtured and not valued. It will feel to me that you've lost your desire to please me, and I will interpret that as you saying you no longer care how I feel. That feeling will eventually turn into anger or resentment, and at some point, I will respond to you in kind: I will start ignoring your requests, and I will be insensitive to your needs or desires also.

We are talking about a basic tenet of how intimate relationships function (and malfunction): show me how important I am to you, and do so frequently. To do otherwise is to let our relationship become withdrawn, detached, and disengaged, which is what happens to a large percentage of relationships over time. Intimate spouses become intimate strangers. They quit trying to please, quit giving as much, quit feeling lucky for having found someone who can be theirs, quit romancing, quit working at it—until one day the relationship has grown empty, void of friendship or depth, disconnected, passionless.

My advice is similar to both women whose letters appear above. You're going to have to tell your man exactly what you need in order to feel like he has skin in the game also, so to speak.

It is not selfish to ask your husband to offer you a sincere and genuine compliment once a day, let alone once a week. If he doesn't want to, he has grown complacent and remote, and he has quit trying to keep the relationship connected and engaged—or perhaps he just doesn't think highly of you anymore. That's when the decision is in your court about exactly how invisible you are willing to be in this marriage.

For the reader who is in a relationship with an ambivalent, passive man who doesn't make much of an effort to show you he values you, I would recommend that you offer him very specific guidance. Tell him what you need for him to do. Don't just complain about what he's not doing; tell him in very clear terms what you need and desire. If he wants the relationship to continue, he will take seriously what you say. If he doesn't, he is saying that you're not all that special to him and that he is not willing to put forth any more effort in order to make the relationship closer.

Love the heart that hurts you, but never hurt the heart that loves you." (Vipin Sharma)

FINDING YOUR VOICE

Dear Neil: My boyfriend and I have been dating for several months. I am in my 20s attending university. He's moving at the end of next month an hour away (I do not have a car), and when he gets another contract, he could be going anywhere. This man is someone I think I love, and I want a long-term relationship with him, but I'm too scared to talk to him about how I feel. He's hard to talk to because he keeps these walls up all the time, and it seems like he's trying to keep it that way. I know he cares about me, but he's holding back, and I don't want to freak him out.

Should I simply walk away from this? I've never been so scared to lose someone.

—Unsure What to Do in Canada

Dear Canada: You're never going to know where you stand with your boyfriend until you can find your voice—and then talk with him.

With that voice it would be appropriate for you to tell him where you would like to see the relationship headed. If you would like to better know where he stands regarding a relationship with you, you could simply ask him. If you would like to express sadness or hurt at him moving farther away from you, you could tell him that. If you would like a greater commitment from him, you could say that—and then let him know what a deeper commitment would entail. Of course, he doesn't have to agree to all of this, but you do get to ask for what you want, and you do get to make requests of him that would help you feel more safe and secure with him.

Relationships require risk, and it may be that he is simply afraid of growing closer to you, or that he doesn't know how to. In that case, perhaps all he needs to hear is some words of encouragement—"I am happy being with you." "You're doing really well with me, do you know that?" "I don't want you to move further away because I want our relationship to go further. How do you feel about that?" It could be that he is holding back because he doesn't feel worthy of a woman's love, or because he's afraid of being rejected. Perhaps all he needs to hear is that you feel close to him and that you would like the relationship to deepen.

Of course, it could also be that he just isn't that into you, as the expression goes. That's the down side of taking such a risk—you risk learning that he doesn't want the relationship any closer, or that he's not willing to be responsive to you or your desires, or that he sees his career as his priority right now.

But learning that, even though it would be painful, would also be liberating. You would then know where you stand, and you could then direct your attention and your energy accordingly. The bottom line is that you're going to have to find your voice and tell him what you want, or you risk losing him—or at least seeing him less frequently.

The odd thing is that you already know your voice. You want a greater commitment, and you want the possibility of a long-term love relationship with him. So it's not that you don't know how you feel or what you want. It's that you're afraid of taking the risk and being rejected, afraid you couldn't tolerate hearing that he doesn't have the same feelings about you that you have about him. So I'll say it again: relationships require risk. No doubt you grew up with adages about this subject, such as "nothing risked, nothing gained."

It would be an act of courage and bravery for you to overcome your fear of rejection—and learn to express what you want in an intimate relationship. By doing so, you would learn how to talk with a man openly and honestly about how you feel, about what you're seeking, about what arrangement would work for you (and what wouldn't), about what he seeks in a relationship, and whether he's ready and interested in a greater commitment. While you're at it, you could even ask him why he seems to be holding back around you, and what would it take for him to take down some of his walls.

If you were to do this, you would learn two things very quickly. The first is whether he wants a closer relationship with you and how ready he is for such a relationship. The second thing you would learn is how to have an effective relationship with a man—and how to take that relationship beyond the superficial and assist it in deepening.

If you can't talk openly and honestly with a man, how are you going to have a good relationship with him?

"It is more fun contemplating someone else's navel than your own."
(Arthur Hoppe)

COUPLE'S EXERCISE IN DEEPENING THE INTIMACY IN YOUR RELATIONSHIP

Have you ever wondered how people deepen the intimacy and closeness in their relationships? Try this exercise, which will allow you to "interview" your spouse or intimate partner—and hopefully assist you in gaining a greater depth of understanding and closeness in your relationship. If you'd like to find out more information about any given subject, ask additional questions—such as how, where, when, how often, how long, likes and dislikes, desires and requests.

Ask your partner how s/he feels about your relationship—and about you—in the following areas:

- Communication
- Hopes, wishes, and dreams
- Fears/anxieties
- What angers you
- Giving affection

- Receiving affection
- Spirituality or religion
- Neatness, cleanliness, and personal hygiene
- Money and financial issues
- The past
- The future
- Children/parenting issues
- Feelings about family, extended family or time spent with family
- Romance
- Sex
- Personal friendships/couple's friendships/time spent with friends
- What irritates you
- What makes you happy
- Interests/hobbies
- Travel/vacations
- Holidays, birthdays, anniversaries, special occasions
- Giving love
- Receiving love
- Entertainment/TV

- Self-improvement
- Dress/clothing/appearance
- Meals/food
- Alcohol or other substances
- Exercise and fitness
- Weight
- Trust
- Time spent together
- Work
- House/home
- Regrets
- Sadnesses
- Apologies
- Requests
- What I could do that would help you to feel closer?

Make sure to take turns asking each other these questions, so it's not one-sided. And don't try to get through these questions all at the same time. It will be more effective and intimate if you take one or several of these questions every few days—and continue this discussion over the course of a month or two. That way the intimacy and connection between the two of you has an opportunity of deepening over time.

"You don't marry one person; you marry three—the person you think they are, the person they are, and the person they are going to become as a result of being married to you." (Richard Needham)

HOW TO ROMANCE A WOMAN

Here's a snap quiz. When women use the term *romance*, what do they mean? What does romance mean to most women? And when men use the term romance, what does *romance* mean to them?

Before you read what I'm about to say, answer the above questions first.

One gender (women) will get the answers to the above questions right, and the other gender (men) will have to think for a while about the questions, and then maybe will or maybe won't get the answers correct.

Men tend to define romance sexually. Women more commonly define romance as words and behaviors that represent that they are loved, cherished, valued, respected, and desired. Although there is some carryover between the two definitions, they're still not the same. Men define romance as the prelude to sex, and women define romance as one of the expressions of love.

So pay attention, gentlemen, because when women feel loved, cherished, valued, respected and desired, they tend to show their appreciation sexually.

Are you following me?

In order for romance to stay alive, you have to keep it alive—it doesn't stay strong by itself. A relationship between once-close lovers will drift apart if both of you don't put effort into keeping the connection, the closeness, the friendliness, and the eroticism alive.

So permit me to address the question of how to romance a woman:

- When you think of nurturing a child, most of us know what that means. But when I ask people about how they nurture their spouse or intimate partner, they frequently give me blank stares, as if they don't quite know what nurturing an adult consists of. Here are some common nurturing behaviors most adults crave: cuddling, being told they are loved, sincere compliments, great food, empathy, compassion, friendship, kindness, expressing an interest in me and how I'm feeling, going out on a date—and affection that doesn't have an expectation attached to it.

- Frequently we expect our relationships to be positive, loving, and responsive while we act upset, angry, rude, or demanding. But people lose respect for those who are rude, inconsiderate, or disrespectful. So no belittling or disrespectful comments or behaviors—to your lady or to anyone else. Always act gentlemanly and respectful.

- Be emotionally safe. This means you must remove your reactivity, defensiveness, anger, hostility, sarcasm, name-calling, and negativity from all communication with your valentine. Being emotionally safe also means that you will refrain from withdrawing in order to get what you want, or from threatening the stability of the relationship.

- Reciprocal sharing is the best type of communication. It's about being interested and inquisitive about your lover's emotions, needs, and desires. It also means that you will be an extremely good listener, and that you can hear your mate's emotions without getting defensive, hostile or dismissive. It's intoxicating to feel that someone is truly interested in what you feel and think.

- Endearments. Whispering "sweet nothings" in her ear. What character traits does she have that you respect or admire? Is she considerate? Trustworthy? A good mother? Compassionate? Sexy? Fun? A good friend? These are the reasons you chose her. Tell her. While you're at it, write your own version of Elizabeth Barrett Browning's poem: "How do I love thee? Let me count the ways…" and give her your answers in writing.

- Express your love physically every day, through touch, hugs, and kisses. Touch helps us to get close, feel close, and stay close. If you're not touching each other a lot, your relationship is unlikely to feel passionate, and both of you will notice that the closeness and connection you once had has waned.

- Emotional presence. Making yourself available and showing up. Having a willingness to share your thoughts, feelings, hopes, hurts, yearnings and fears—and to truly hear hers.

- Flowers, cards, notes, surprises, weekend getaways, sweet texts, voice mail, or email messages, doing something to lighten her load or relieve her of some of her chores—these romantic gestures matter. If these gestures stop, courtship will stop, and then your relationship risks growing stale. So no matter how long you may have been married, woo her.

"No matter how happily a woman may be married, it always pleases her to discover that there is a nice man who wishes she were not." (H. L. Mencken)

DEEPENING THE CONNECTION IN A NEW RELATIONSHIP

Most people find the meeting, dating, getting-to-know-you stage of a relationship awkward and uncomfortable. Even though there is the potential for romance, sex, love, and "happily ever after" (or maybe because there is that potential), people ranging in age from teens to senior citizens find themselves nervously tripping over their words while trying to initiate greater closeness in a promising new relationship.

If you're in that situation, worry no more. If done with a co-participant who is willing to be open and honest, the following questions/topics are designed to help you deepen the connection and closeness between the two of you.

Ask each other the following questions. Be as thorough as possible with each question because short and superficial responses will not help you learn about each other, and then the relationship will be less likely to grow deeper and more intimate. Expect multiple answers to every question.

Do you fall in love readily and quickly, or do you tend to hold back?

Do you see yourself as easy to get to know or hard to get to know?

Do you see yourself as defensive?

Are you uncomfortable with negative feedback, constructive criticism, or requests for a change of behavior? If so, how am I going to have a voice around you and speak up when I'm unhappy?

How would you like us to handle it when we have a major disagreement? What behaviors are unacceptable in a fight?

Are you happy in your work? Thinking about a career change? When do you see yourself as retiring, and what do you envision you'll be doing in retirement?

What dreams or goals would you like to accomplish or experience before you die?

In one sentence, describe yourself. Describe me.

Are you quick to anger? Do you have a short fuse? How is it best to respond to you when you're upset, irritable, or angry? What should I not do? How do I disarm you when you're angry?

Do you avoid conflicts? What issues do you have a hard time dealing with? How would you like me to approach you if I feel you're ignoring or avoiding something?

How have you contributed to the difficulties in your previous relationships? What was your role in assisting those relationships to fail? (Talk about your contribution to the relationship souring, not your ex-partner's role.)

What helps you stay connected? What lessens the connection for you? When the connection is lower, what will you do to help us repair wounded feelings so we can reconnect?

How trusting of people are you? What generates mistrust? What behaviors would you consider to be a violation of your trust? Do you ever get jealous or mistrusting without good cause? What would you like me to do if that happens?

Can you describe what an extremely romantic evening for you would consist of? What would make this an extremely romantic relationship?

What money habits do you have that reasonably could be called unhealthy? How should we deal with money disputes or with different financial priorities?

How important is it to you that we have frequent sex? What does good sex consist of?

How important is fidelity to you—yours and mine?

What issues have dominated your previous relationships? (The fight for control? Power struggles? Mistrust? Infidelity? Dishonesty? Lack of common interests? Withdrawal? Lack of time spent together? Poor communication? Withdrawal of sex? Children or child rearing? Money disputes? Betrayals? What have your biggest relationship headaches been about?)

What relationships issues are you most fearful of encountering again?

Is there anything about me that you find annoying, irritating, difficult or challenging—or that you're not sure you can handle? Be truthful.

"All women's dresses are merely variations on the eternal struggle between the admitted desire to dress and the unadmitted desire to undress." (Lin Yutang)

HOW DOES A COUPLE DEEPEN A RELATIONSHIP?

Dear Neil: I have lived with my boyfriend for ten months. A couple of weeks ago he went out with a long-time female friend of his, and he didn't get home until 3 a.m. on a Tuesday night. I questioned him about where he was, and he said "at a bar," which I later found out doesn't open on Tuesday night.

I don't question his faithfulness; it is the dishonesty that has affected me so much. Why lie to me? I have asked him to tell me if he feels confident about a future together, and he is unsure. I am now feeling very anxious, like I'm "on trial." Can you recommend how to deal with this knowing that the relationship may be over?

—Anxious In New Zealand

Dear Anxious: You sound as if your boyfriend is the only person who must make a choice about the future of the relationship. But that is not so. You both have to decide if there are enough positives to outweigh the negatives—enough warmth, affection, friendship, respect and love to sustain the relationship over time.

Even if your answer is "yes," don't give away what's in ant to you. Two people committed to each other agree on cer ain codes of behavior they both are willing to live by, and your relationship is being forced to create such agreements. So address the following questions together.

- What are your expectations about sexual fidelity? About opposite-sex friendships? About honesty? About when and under which circumstances it's okay to mislead or deceive the other person? When one person is going to be late, is that person responsible for letting the other know who they're with and where they are?
- Are you agreeing to be a team—facing the world together—or are you agreeing to be two separate individuals functioning more or less independently of each other? When are you answerable to the other person? Are both partner's input about major decisions solicited and considered important, or are decisions made unilaterally?
- How do you want me to show that I love and value you? Are you committed to me? Are you committed to each other? What does that commitment mean, exactly, and how solid is it? Do you like me? Accept me? Respect me? Value my contribution...If not, specifically what do you want different?

The disagreement between you and your boyfriend does not mean that your relationship needs to end. It means that your partnership needs to deepen, and that the two of you need to be talking about what kind of relationship you're trying to have and how you expect to achieve such a relationship. For instance, you wonder why he lied to you instead of telling you the truth. Why don't you ask him?

If your boyfriend refuses to address these questions—or if his commitment remains as lukewarm as it now is—or if his deceptive or dishonest behavior continues, then it would be wise for you to leave him. You don't want to communicate that he can do anything he wants and then lie to you about it. That will set you up for being permanently anxious, insecure, and miserable with him.

"Unfortunately, this world is full of people who are ready to think the worst when they see a man sneaking out of the wrong bedroom in the middle of the night." (Will Cuppy)

DEEPENING A RELATIONSHIP TAKES EFFORT

The following is a continuation of ideas about how to deepen a relationship. Take turns talking together about your feelings, concerns, wishes, and expectations regarding:

- How much effort do you expect each person to give to the relationship? How should it be dealt with if one person feels the other isn't making much of an effort?
- What's fun to you? How could you expand your notion of what's fun? What role should having fun or play have in your relationship on a daily/weekly/monthly basis?
- What helps you to feel loved, valued, and cared for? What assists you in feeling close and connected? What interferes?
- What priority are travel and vacations to you? The frequency of travel? Where you wish to travel?
- How important are neatness, cleanliness, appearance, and personal hygiene to you—yours and mine? Are there any changes you would like us to make in this regard?

- What priority does work take in your life? What priority should it take? What happens when one person feels the other is too consumed by work—or that the relationship is becoming subordinate to and less important than work?

- When you become crabby, irritable, short-tempered, or hard to be around, what would you like me to say or do? What should I not say or do?

- If there are children/grandchildren in your life—or if you're wanting there to be children in your future—what role would you like me to play? How would you like disagreements to be resolved about how to parent or how to discipline?

- How trusting of other people do you think you are? How trusting do you think I am? What behaviors would violate trust? To what extent do we have to continually prove that we're trustworthy to each other? What needs to happen if trust were ever to be ruptured in our relationship?

- How would you like holidays, birthdays, anniversaries, and special occasions to be honored?

- What would you like to see happen if ever there was a breakdown in communication or if the connection between the two of us were to become weaker?

- How important is daily nonsexual affection to you? What is the right balance between the giving and receiving of affection? How should it be handled if affection were to become strained or diminished?

- What role does spirituality play in our relationship? What role would you like it to play?

- Have your previous intimate relationships had major trust issues? How about issues around control? Honesty? Fidelity? Integrity? Sex? Money? Children? Family? Common interests? Time spent together? Poor communication? Loss of connection? If any of these issues were to become important in this relationship, how would you like them to be handled?
- Who's primarily responsible for household chores (cooking, dishes, laundry, childcare, keeping the house straightened up and clean, shopping, yard work, etc.)? How do you want these tasks to be allocated?
- What are your feelings about sex, including frequency, fidelity, what's desirable, what's undesirable, and what's forbidden?

"People who throw kisses are hopelessly lazy." (Bob Hope)

CHRONIC COMPLAINERS DEADEN THE INTIMACY IN THEIR RELATIONSHIP

Dear Neil: I live with a man who is driving me crazy. Seemingly, he's unhappy about almost everything—his job, the amount of money he makes, how much he has saved for retirement, how other people treat him, how his kids are ungrateful for all he has done for them, about his hurt knee, his wounded pride because his last employer let him go, how unfair things are that he hasn't traveled as much as he's desired. He's unhappy with his lot in life, and feels cheated. This causes me endless frustration, and it's becoming increasingly difficult to be around him. Help.

—Needing Help in British Columbia

Dear Needing Help: Chronic complaining eats away at the fabric of a relationship. It puts one person in the position of repeatedly attempting to fix the problems or emotions of another. In a relationship, all of us occasionally ask that our partners help us fix a problem and repair our emotions. That's one of the benefits of being in a relationship.

But even if the partner of a chronic complainer is extraordinary compassionate and empathetic, over time that person is likely to develop compassion fatigue. That is, you'll grow weary of repeatedly listening to the misery, the suffering, the "woe is me" attitude—and you'll wind up tuning your partner's complaints out, becoming more and more deaf to that which you can't fix and what just drags you down.

It's a downer to listen to someone you care about chronically unhappy or miserable. It's disempowering for both of you, and over any period time, both of you will likely to grow hopeless and despondent. Worst of all, it deadens the intimacy in your relationship. How intimate do you think you're going to feel when your intimate partner communicates that s/he is unhappy the vast majority of the time?

If you're a chronic complainer, the only lasting solution is to get very proactive and aggressively fix the issues causing your unhappiness. As best you can, one by one, tackle and defeat every injustice, disappointment, disillusionment or hurt you feel. By consistently being constructive in trying to get your life back on track, you'll increase your self-esteem and your self-confidence.

If you are the partner of a chronic complainer, understand that he is hoping for a compassionate and caring companion who will rescue him from his misery and help him to be happier.

But you're going to have to set boundaries and put limits on how much caring and compassion you're willing to offer. So ask your partner what he can do to constructively address or resolve his problems or worries, and then encourage him to take action. Communicate to him that you believe in him—and that you know he's capable of solving the issue. Perhaps you might offer your help so the two of you work as a team to help resolve what's bothering him. But nothing will change if he is unwilling to take constructive action on his own behalf.

HOW DO I STOP BEING JEALOUS AND POSSESSIVE?

Dear Neil: My boyfriend and I are now in our fifth year. Ever since we started our relationship, we have been very attached. We were always together or constantly texting each other. I'm twenty-four and he's twenty-six. Two years ago, I cheated on him, and he found out. Yet he still accepted me, and he's made a way for us to be okay and to move on.

Then I started to be possessive: I'd get jealous of his classmates and friends (most of his friends are females). I started to be clingy and possessive, to the point where I began to look like an investigator or a spy. I feel like all of his time should be focused on me, which is how we were in the beginning of our relationship.

I know that the mistake is on me, and that we should both have our own lives. But I'm confused about what I should do in order to prevent him from falling out of love with me.

—Clingy Girlfriend

Dear Clingy: You are insecure and clingy because you are making the assumption that you are not worthy of being loved. In essence, you do not feel deserving of love, fidelity, and commitment from your boyfriend. As a result, you are assuming yo is going to fall out of love with you, and eventually dı another woman.

So no wonder you are clingy, possessive, and insecure. And it certainly doesn't help that you are five years into a relationship and the chemistry that defined your early relationship has waned a bit, like it does for everyone. You also may be assuming that because you cheated, so could he—which is making you jealous and threatened by his friendships and dealings with other women.

Here's what you could do in order to give yourself an opportunity to live more in peace—and for your relationship to become more stable and secure. First, you need way more reassurance than you are getting. So ask your boyfriend to reassure you every day, by saying something like: "What I like about you is ..." "What I love about you is ..." "I respect that you ..." "Some of your best qualities are ..." and "What I like so much about our relationship is ...."

You (and he) could add other things that would help you to feel reassured, but be sure to tell him what you like, love, and respect about him as well—because he may also need reassurance that you're not going to step out on him again. You might find being held or cuddled to be reassuring as well.

Now comes the hard part: you're going to have to improve your feelings of self-worth and the feelings that you aren't worthy of love and fidelity. Find a psychotherapist that specializes in self-esteem, and buy some books (and work the exercises) on how people improve self-esteem. Without that, you will forever fear your boyfriend is going to dump you for another woman, and you will be more likely to push him away by clinging too hard.

One other thing. You are focused on him, who he's with, and what he's doing too much, and not enough on yourself. Find interests, hobbies, classes, hikes, or other activities that will occupy your time when you are alone.

WHAT ARE YOUR HOT-BUTTON ISSUES?

What sets you off? Are there predictable land mines that trigger fights, arguments or angry outbursts—in your intimate relationship, with your children or with other close people to you? Here are a list of hot-button issues and emotional triggers, many of which come from Ellen Wachtel in her book *We Love Each Other, But …* (St. Martin's Griffin). Which of these describe you, your partner, or your intimate relationship?

- Do you tend to feel that you are not the number one priority in your partner's life?
- Do you feel hurt easily?
- Do you like things "just so"? Is it hard for you to see things done the "wrong" way? Is it hard for you to delegate responsibility to someone else?
- Are you afraid of too much closeness or dependency? Do you keep yourself removed, walled off, uninvolved or largely unavailable?

- Do you fear abandonment? Can you easily feel neglected or slighted?
- Do you get jealous easily?
- Do you tend to feel that you are being taken advantage of?
- Are you more critical than you would like to be?
- Do you get impatient easily? Do you speak with an edge in your voice when you think your partner should already know something or when she repeats herself?
- Do you tend to see the glass as half empty rather than half full?
- Do you have difficulty relaxing until everything on your day's "to do" list is accomplished? Are you a bit compulsive?
- Are you overly sensitive to criticism?
- Do you worry about being controlled?
- Do you have difficulty saying "no" and therefore get overextended? Do you push yourself to the point of getting overwhelmed?
- Do you revisit decisions over and over again that have already been made?
- Do you mull over what is bothering you for a long time before expressing your feelings?
- Do you blame or lash out when you are frustrated?
- Are you stubborn?
- Are you moody?

- Do you have trouble admitting to or apologizing when you are wrong?
- Do you interpret your partner's clutter and mess in the house to mean that s/he does not care about what is important to you?
- Do you feel you give a great deal more than you receive from your partner?
- Do you feel your partner lacks empathy or is unresponsive to your feelings, needs, or desires? Do you feel that your partner doesn't treat your desires as important?
- Do you have poor control over your anger, reactivity, defensiveness, anxiety, or fear?
- Do you feel your efforts go unappreciated by your partner?
- Do you feel badly treated or poorly respected by your partner?
- Are you craving more nurturing, friendliness, affection, tenderness, or sex?
- Do you feel betrayed?
- Is there secrecy, withholding of personal information or dishonesty in your relationship?
- Are you reluctant to commit?

"I love being married. It's so great to find one special person you want to annoy for the rest of your life." (Rita Rudner)

WHAT ARE YOUR FIGHTS REALLY ABOUT? PART 1

Have you ever had a huge argument over something completely trivial and minor? Remember the feeling you had afterwards—embarrassment that you let something so insignificant completely take you over?

Think again. Your argument may not have been so minor after all. You just weren't verbalizing the real issue correctly. Many of us have heard the reports that say most couples fight over things such as money, sex, or children. But I'm not talking about the subject you fight about. I'm more interested in what you're really fighting about—which may not be the actual subject of your fight. Follow me so far?

OK, I'll explain. Sometimes what a fight is about (let's say messiness around the house) isn't what you're really fighting about. What you may actually be fighting about is that your partner isn't pulling his/her fair share around the house, which imposes a greater burden on you. But messiness triggers the issue, so the two of you engage in a knock-down, drag-out fight about messiness, completely missing the far more important subterranean issue that was really driving the fight. That is what normally happens f us: what triggers our fights may not be the real issue that we're actually upset about—and it may not be spoken even during the fight.

I have compiled some of the fights couples engage in, and will try to translate for you what I think they're actually fighting about:

FIGHT: Occasionally you fly into a jealous rage, accusing your partner of behaviors or motives that you consider treason.

REAL ISSUE: You need more reassurance that your partner is committed to you and isn't looking for someone else. You may also have an insecurity or a self-worth issue—and therefore feel you're not worthy of your partner—which means you need a great deal more reassurance, pampering, romance, endearments, or affection.

FIGHT: Your partner isn't paying bills on time, and paying the household bills is one of his/her jobs.

REAL ISSUE: Trust. Can I trust you to care for us, and not do things that will injure us?

FIGHT: Your partner is getting drunk (or high) a lot.

REAL ISSUE: Your partner (and therefore the relationship) feels unsafe, unreliable, and unstable to you. You may also be fearful of losing respect or trust for him/her.

FIGHT: Your partner is working too much.

REAL ISSUE: S/he's not making you a high enough priority. S/he is not spending enough time with you for you to feel wanted, valued, and cherished. You want more time made available for you or for the family.

FIGHT: Your partner has withdrawn sexually, and is much less interested than she was before.

REAL ISSUE: The relationship isn't reciprocal. I'm giving more than I'm getting. I'm heavily contributing to her happiness and wellbeing, but s/he isn't taking an interest in mine.

FIGHT: He talks about how hot other women are.

REAL ISSUE: You feel inadequate around him. You feel he's negatively comparing you to other women, and that makes you feel far less secure and desirable.

FIGHT: She is shopping a lot, and your joint financial resources are extremely limited.

REAL ISSUE: You feel your partner is being selfish and self-absorbed and is not looking out for you—or for what is best for the relationship.

Nothing is a greater impediment to being on good terms with others than being ill at ease with yourself." (Honore de Balzac)

WHAT ARE YOUR FIGHTS REALLY ABOUT? PART 2

Think for a moment. What triggers the fights in your relationship? Do minor things build up until they explode? Do ongoing conflicts erupt from time to time? Are there rude little jabs or sarcastic responses? Or perhaps it is name calling, disrespectful or mean-spirited behaviors, the cold silent treatment or your partner's refusal to talk with you that feels so provocative and aggravating? Maybe it's the accumulation of a number of slights—both large and small—that make you feel that you're not respected or valued?

When you're in a fight with an intimate partner, do you usually know exactly what it is that you're fighting for? How confident are you that you fully understand what your partner is fighting for—and what triggers him or her?

Following is a continuation of couple's conflicts and issues, and what you and your partner may actually be fighting for:

FIGHT: Your partner repeatedly loses control of his/her temper and blows up at you.

REAL ISSUE: Safety. Is it safe for me to be around you?

FIGHT: He got home two hours late and didn't call ahead of time.

REAL ISSUE: Respect. How important am I to you? Where do I fit in as a priority in your life?

FIGHT: You decide the furniture needs to be replaced, and your partner resists.

REAL ISSUE: Power struggle/control issue. Who calls the shots around here? Whose rules are we agreeing to live by? There may also be an additional issue of one person feeling that the other one is acting unilaterally and not as part of a team.

FIGHT: You discover he has been visiting Internet porn sites.

REAL ISSUE: Trust and betrayal. There are certain things that feel sacred in a relationship, and this may feel like a betrayal, because he clearly must not be happy or satisfied with you.

FIGHT: You asked her to watch her spending of money and to keep it under control, but she was frivolous and excessive instead.

REAL ISSUE: You don't feel she's got your best interests at heart, and you don't feel important or valued by her. She's ignoring what you said mattered to you, and she isn't honoring your needs or wishes—and she may be jeopardizing your financial stability.

FIGHT: Differing sexual appetites. You want to make love considerably more frequently than your partner does.

REAL ISSUE: Do I have to give up me and what matters to me in order to be with you? Can't you give me what I want? Plus, your partner isn't treating your needs and wishes as important.

FIGHT: He is either working, or on the computer or watching TV, and therefore has very little time for you.

REAL ISSUE: Things are too distant. We're not close enough, and I want more than you're giving. Plus, how important am I to you, anyway?

FIGHT: You discover that she's gotten very chummy with a male co-worker, and they've met for drinks after work several times.

REAL ISSUE: Trust and the fear of betrayal. Can I trust that you're mine and that I don't have to worry that you're looking to leave me? Plus, you're not keeping me informed about what you're doing. You are also feeling powerless and out of control.

"When you meet a man, don't you always idly wonder what he'd be like in bed? I do." (Helen Gurley Brown)

A COUPLE'S EXERCISE TO EFFECTIVELY RESOLVE CONFLICT

Imagine the following scenario: Someone close to you gets in an accident and winds up with a broken nose. Her nose healed, but she remains fearful of being seen in public. She says her nose doesn't look right, and she doesn't want anyone to see her, so she stays home virtually all the time. You're in the position of encouraging her to get out of the house and resume her normal life.

Which of the following comes closest to how you would handle the situation: (A) "Your nose is fine. This fear you have is all in your head." (B) "I'm going to go out, and if you want to stay home and feel sorry for yourself, you can just be miserable for as long as you want." (C) "I see that you feel people will be critical and judgmental of your appearance, and I might feel the same way if what happened to you had happened to me. This must feel terrible, and I can identify with how disempowered you must feel. Tell me more about these feelings."

There is no universally correct answer to the above question. But the answer that is most likely to work with the most people is (C), because (C) is the only answer that employs empathy—attempting to understand the feelings, motivations, and fears of the other person.

Empathy is a skill, and few people are really good at it. It requires us to step into another's shoes and imagine what it must feel like to be in his/her position. It invites us to enter into the other person's feelings as if those feelings are ours.

Empathy is not the same as sympathy. I feel sympathy for you when something bad happens to you. I feel empathy when I feel with you, when I feel what you're feeling from your perspective, and by having a genuine, non-judgmental desire to understand your feelings.

To have empathy does not mean that if you're angry at someone, I will be also. It just means that I can understand and have compassion for what you're feeling, even if I don't have those feelings myself, and even if I disagree with you.

Empathy is a healing emotion, because when people feel heard and understood, they also feel validated, which will helps them to feel better. They'll suddenly feel like they're not all alone.

Empathy consists of (1) finding the truth in what the other person says, (2) paraphrasing the other person's words to make sure you understand his/her feelings accurately, (3) acknowledging what it must feel like to be in his/her position, and (4) having a willingness to take yourself—your thoughts, feelings and judgments—out of the mix and just be there with the other person. If the other person is upset with me, than there's a fifth step if I want to help fix the problem or resolve the issue: it's about asking the question: "What can I do to eliminate or reduce these issues or to assist you in feeling better?"

If you don't temporarily suspend your own feelings and opinions, you're not being empathetic. If you tell me, for example, that you're upset at your boss, it doesn't help for me to tell you how upset

I am with my boss, or even how upset I am with your b that, my emotions are about my feelings, not about your feelings.

Author's Harville Hendrix and Helen LaKelly Hunt offer the following "frustration dialogue" exercise if you're interested in learning and/or getting better at attempting to resolve conflicts or issues with your partner/spouse :

Sender: Speaks of his/her emotions or frustrations.

You: "If I understand you, you're feeling…" or "You're saying you're feeling…" You are paraphrasing your partner's emotions, not mimicking or parroting. This is very important. Paraphrasing indicates that you understand what your partner is saying, because you're saying it back in your own words. Mimicking or parroting can feel as if you're being mocking.

Sender: Confirms the message was received accurately (or re-phrases message if not received accurately).

You: "Is there more about that?" This question continues until the sender is able to say everything important about the frustration, which may take many answers. Be patient—you're doing perhaps the single most loving thing you can do for your partner/spouse. You're letting him or her express strong emotions safely, and you are creating a loving and caring environment for him/her to express everything s/he feels. When your partner has expressed all answers to the question, the sender continues with a second question.

Sender: "What I'm afraid of is …"

You: Paraphrase in the same way as above. (You don't have to agree with your partner or feel the same way as s/he does, but you're assisting him/her to get all these emotions out—and you're making it feel safe to do so.)

Sender: What hurts so much about this is …"

You: Paraphrase back the messages you hear, until your partner has had an opportunity to express all answers to this question.

Sender: "What this reminds me of from my past (or my childhood) is ..."

You: Paraphrase back the messages you hear.

You: Express validation and empathy for the other person's feelings. Validation and empathy does not mean agreement. I can be validating and empathetic of your quandary and still think you acted poorly or made a bad decision. To validate, you can use such phrases as "I can understand why you feel this way because..." or "This makes sense because ..."

To express empathy, try "If what happened to you had happened to me, I would feel...." Or "If I felt the way you feel, I would feel ..." (Or some variation similar to that.)

Sender: "Ideally ..." (Given reality, this is inviting the sender to dream out-loud about what s/he would like to happen, or what s/he would like you to do to ease the problem.)

You: Paraphrase back everything you hear.

Sender: Makes two requests of you that you could reasonability do (or begin doing) in the next two weeks or so. These requests need to be positive, measurable, and specific. (Therefore "Be nicer to me" is not effective, because there's that's not specific enough in order for the two of you to be able to agree on that that means. However, " I would like a kiss and an embrace before you leave the house in the morning, and another one when you come back" is specific and measurable. Likewise "I would like more affection" is not as effective as "I would like us to cuddle every night before we go to sleep.")

You: Agree to the two requests if you can. If you can't agree with how they're currently worded, you can change, tweak, or modify the requests any way you would like. But understand that the purpose of this exercise is to help your partner/spouse feel better, and that you're agreeing to a two-week trial—not for the rest of your life.

After this dialogue has ended, it becomes your turn to present a problem or a frustration in the same way, reversing roles so the you are now the speaker and your partner/spouse is now person receiving your emotions, paraphrasing the meaning of what you're saying, offering validation and empathy, and hopefully agreeing to two solutions that would fix, resolve, or at least greatly reduce your frustration, issue or problem.

Two weeks later, it is important that the two of you revisit the issues and the solutions presented—and review whether each person lived up to his/her agreements. If not, recommit to the two requests again, this time writing your agreement down on a note where you stick it on your computer or your vanity mirror—or some other place where you will be reminded of it multiple times a day, every day.

Conversely, either of you can change the requests (with your partner's agreement), because your goal is to defeat the issue bothering you—and whatever works to achieve that goal is more important than how you get there.

"Of all forms of caution, caution in love is perhaps the most fatal to true happiness." (Bertrand Russell)

WHAT ARE THE DEAL-BREAKERS IN YOUR RELATIONSHIP?

Dear Neil: You usually write about how people can stay together and work out their differences. But what about when it may not be in your self-interest to stay, or when you have an extremely unresponsive, uncaring, or hurtful partner? Could you talk about how to decide when it is time to cut and run?

—Feeling the Heat in Delaware

Dear Feeling the Heat: The following are guidelines about how to decide which of your issues are relationship deal breakers—and when you'd be better off out of the relationship rather than in it:

- **Your partner has a wall up around himself.** He doesn't let himself get too involved, too close, or intimate, too dependent, too emotionally available, or too vulnerable to you. He's cautious, held back, reserved. He may have a major fear of being hurt, so he has grown afraid of deep closeness or connection. He may feel pretty emotionally beaten up from his previous intimate life experiences and has all but given up on the dream of loving or of being loved.

- **She puts very little of herself into the relationship.** She simply doesn't try very hard, doesn't give very much effort or time, and doesn't give much of herself.
- **There's too much of him and not enough you (or "we").** Both of you are looking to meet his needs. There isn't a reciprocal effort to look out for you.
- **She has poor control over her reactivity, defensiveness, anxiety or fear.** Those emotions rule her—and therefore control your relationship.
- **Your partner focuses on what he doesn't like.** The focus is on what annoys him, what angers him or what he feels judgmental or critical about—and he tends to minimize or ignore the thoughtful, caring, loving things you do or you offer.
- **You fear setting her off.** You walk on eggshells a large amount of the time, because her reactions are so severe or volatile that you find it next to impossible to express your concerns, wishes, annoyances, needs, or requests.
- **It feels that you care about/love him more than he loves you.**
- **She lacks empathy for your feelings, your needs or your desires.** She isn't responsive to what you say you want. She wants to give what she feels like giving, not what you say you want or need.
- **You feel mistrusted a lot.** You're in the position of having to prove your trustworthiness over and over again. (If you've

earned this mistrust, this is required. If you haven't earned it, this becomes increasingly intolerable.)

- **You've been waiting a long time for him to not put work first, or to quit drinking, or to communicate better, or to be kinder to the kids.** You know that if these traits or behaviors don't improve, you'll never be happy with him.
- **You put more effort into the relationship than she does.** You're trying harder than she is to make the relationship closer, warmer, more connected, more trusting, or to fix the problems in the relationship.

"Marriage is a great institution, but I'm not ready for an institution yet." (Mae West)

DO YOU HAVE RELATIONSHIP DEAL-BREAKERS?

The following are a continuation of the guidelines for how to decide which of your issues are deal-breakers—and when you'd be better off leaving a relationship instead of staying in it:

- **When you feel poorly treated.** Poor treatment can come in many forms: disrespectful behavior; knee-jerk reactivity; too much anger, mistrust, or jealousy; or not enough TLC, nurturance, and affection—to name a few. Poor treatment almost always entails one person not valuing how the other person feels and therefore not behaving in ways that allow you to feel cherished, valued and respected.

- **Very little affection and/or sex.** Affection and sex are the glue that keeps couple's feeling close and connected with each other. Ditto if you are no longer sexually attracted to your partner—or your partner has no real sexual interest in you—and you find that intolerable.

- **Dishonesty/lack of trust.** It's hard to trust someone who doesn't act trustworthy—or who has deceived, misled or betrayed you in the past—or who is secretive, hidden, or withholding of personal information.

- **Infidelity or betrayal.** The deception and sense of violation lead to continuing mistrust—and mistrust destroys intimacy.
- **Being resentful, angry or hostile.** Using hurtful, insensitive or demeaning words (or behaviors). If that happens, you will want to avoid your partner, or you or will become afraid of her.
- **Addictions.** You can be addicted to a substance (alcohol, drugs, food), a behavior (watching TV, sleeping, porn, knee-jerk reactivity, jealousy), or an attitude (unwarranted mistrust or suspiciousness, fear of abandonment, selfishness, lack of reciprocity). Any unhealthy addiction will undermine a couple's connection and distance a relationship.
- **Control/power struggles.** This might be related to a self-absorbed, insecure controlling person who wants everything her way, or it might indicate that the two of you have different goals and are therefore fighting for different things. If one person demands that things are done his way, you may feel you have to give yourself up in order to keep the relationship together, which will lead to enormous resentment over time.
- **You no longer have much fun together.** You don't have common goals or interests, so you increasingly find yourself feeling alone and lonely in the relationship.
- **Poor intimacy skills.** Effective relationship skills include give and take communication; being a good listener; knowing how to deal with conflict and differences, compromise, benefit of the doubt, absence of malice, affection and romance.

QUIZ: ARE YOU WALLED OFF ?

Do you have a guarded heart? Do you have a wall around your heart that prohibits genuine intimacy, even with the people you love and feel closest to?

Take this quiz to find out:

- Do you get angry a lot with your mate, even over small things?
- Are you frequently sarcastic?
- Are you having an affair, or looking for one, or do you have a history of affairs?
- Do you tend to focus on your mate's shortcomings or bad traits?
- Do you judge or criticize your spouse for making mistakes, or do you use mistakes as leverage against him/her?
- Do you have the tendency of pushing away intimacy and closeness when it's offered to you but then want it when it's not offered?

- Have you been accused by your partner (or by a previous partner) of being emotionally unavailable, remote, or hard to be close to?
- Are you insecure?
- Do you have a difficult time trusting?
- Do you tend to be emotionally hidden in your relationships, fearing that you'll be discovered as inadequate?
- Do you not have close friends (other than your spouse or family)?
- Do you have a fear of being controlled or of losing your identify in a relationship?
- Do you have a fear of getting rejected, abandoned or betrayed in a relationship?
- Do you tend to put your mate in second or third position a lot?
- Are you critical or judgmental of other people, such as your family, friends, or co-workers?
- Do you take constructive criticism from your mate poorly?
- Do you have a strong fear of being judged or criticized?
- Do you have a fear of being vulnerable or defenseless in a relationship?
- Do you have a history of repeatedly getting involved with emotionally standoffish, disapproving, or angry people?
- Do you often get mean, punishing, or vindictive when you're upset?

- Do you tend to give money, financial support, or sex to show your love?
- Do you have trouble being compassionate or empathetic to your partner?
- Would your partner say that you don't give the relationship a lot of effort?
- Do you have a pattern of withdrawing from people?
- Do you tend to put work (sports, hobbies) above all else?
- Do you drink too much, watch too much TV, worry too much, or have an addiction to any substance?
- Do you sometimes push your partner away because you don't wish to be dependent or beholden?
- Would your partner say that you act or talk disrespectfully to him/her?
- Do you have the vague sense that you repeatedly sabotage love?

If you answered "yes" to ten or more of these questions, you are what I would call emotionally walled off. If you answered "yes" to more than fifteen of these questions, your wall is so thick and impenetrable that the chances of you having a close loving relationship are dramatically diminished.

Relationships die of emotional malnutrition. Make sure you are not being safe at the expense of being happy.

"I honestly believe there is nothing like going to bed with a good book. Or a friend who's read one." (Phyllis Diller)

HOW DO I LET MY GUARD DOWN?

Dear Neil: I grew up believing I had to be strong. I had a difficult childhood and grew up really fast. I never received the nurturance I needed, but I often took care of other family members. I believed I was very strong, but now I realize I am very guarded. I survived my childhood and have an adult life I am very grateful for. I have a good education, have traveled the world with my job, and have amazing friends. I no longer need to be guarded to protect myself from abusive parents and a rough neighborhood. I was able to succeed in so many areas of my life, but I continue to remain very guarded, and as a result, I cannot have an intimate relationship. I used to think that this was because there were no good men around, but I am now realizing that it is not them; it's me. It's not that there are no men who want to date me; I just don't let my guard down, and I won't let a man in. I want to change this, but I don't know how.

—Can't let my guard down in New Jersey

Dear New Jersey: "Distant intimacy" is about being in a relationship with a guarded heart. It allows you to keep your emotional armor in place so you don't get hurt if things don't work out. You want this much safety, because you're afraid of being rejected, betrayed, abused, or controlled or of losing yourself in a relationship—and you're afraid of repeating your childhood if you aren't "strong." Another way of saying that: being emotionally aloof makes you feel less vulnerable, and therefore stronger. So you aren't permitting yourself a deep personal investment with men, which gives you the feeling of safety but not closeness or connection.

The problem is that "intimacy from a distance" isn't very satisfying, because there is so much less emotion, intensity, passion, engagement, and heart. And there is truth to that old adage that says "nothing risked, nothing gained." A passionate and engaged intimate relationship requires of us that we risk our hearts, thereby giving someone else the power to hurt, betray, or reject us.

So what can you do? Plenty, if you're willing to take the risk. You could, for instance, look at:

How do you avoid emotional contact with men? Do you put off contact, withdraw yourself from connection, keep yourself extremely busy so you don't have time for someone else, not bother with trying to look attractive and appealing, or do you keep yourself socially insulated so you don't meet other people? It's very useful to pay close attention to how you avoid contact with men, so if you want to make some changes you'll know where to begin.

What would allow you to feel comfortable with giving love? Comfortable with receiving it? With giving and receiving affection? This is a bigger question than you may suspect. It deserves your full in-depth attention.

What would a man that you were romantically interested in need to do in order for you to feel safe enough to express your tender emotions and reveal your vulnerabilities? How could he help you feel safe?

How would you make time for an intimate relationship? Where would a man fit into your life and your schedule? How could you free up more time in order to be together with someone?

How skilled are you in dealing with conflicts, disagreements, and requests? How well do you handle constructive criticism or critical comments? How defensive are you? How reactive do you get? How respectful are you in a disagreement? What could you do in order to improve in this realm?

In a relationship, how well do you speak up about your wants and needs? What would assist you in being assertive about these without being aggressive or disrespectful?

Look at your abandonment issues: the fears you have about being left, betrayed, rejected or being found not good enough.

Examine your feelings about not feeling worthy of a close love relationship, and your fears that if a man really gets to know you, he won't want you and will eventually reject you. If deep down you don't feel you deserve to be loved and spoiled, you are far more likely to choose a man who you think is unworthy of you, or you will choose a man who can't or won't love you, or you'll run away from anyone who begins to get close to you.

Where could you go and what could you do to make yourself available to new people socially? If you do make yourself socially available, don't be passive. Don't wait for a man to extend a hand—reach out yourself.

Ask yourself this question: If I were going to make my next relationship work, what would I have to do differently? What would I have to stop doing? How could I take more responsibility for meeting men, and for making a relationship closer, more connected and more intimate?

"Love is an ideal thing, marriage is a real thing; a confusion of the real with the ideal never goes unpunished."
(Johann Wolfgang Von Goethe)

LOVE REQUIRES YOU OFFERING YOUR HEART

Dear Neil: In the past few years, I have had several different relationships that seem to follow the same pattern. The man is hot, and the relationship starts out with great interest, enthusiasm, hope, chemistry, and passion. But after a while, I seem to lose that enthusiasm and begin to notice a variety of differences between us: we like different music, have different interests, different political viewpoints, different styles of behaving, different ways of looking at things.

I have been repeatedly told how attractive and sexually appealing I am, and I have had men fall for me hard. But I don't have the same feelings for them that they feel for me, so eventually I wind up ending our relationship. I know I've hurt men badly, but I'm not trying to. I'm looking to fall in love, but it doesn't happen. Why? With all these men who offer love, shouldn't some of this help me in loving them back?

—No Love in London, England

Dear No Love: You're not recognizing that love isn't out there, in men. It's in you.

Someone else, no matter how hot, isn't going to make you fall in love. Only you can do that—what you share of yourself, what you give, what you feel, what you offer. It's about you opening up and giving your heart, sharing your world, your history, your vulnerabilities and sensitivities, your disappointments, hopes, dreams and goals—and also being interested in his.

You falling in love has far less to do with the man than most men would be comfortable in knowing. Your love is not about, and not dependent on, what is attractive, appealing, or wonderful about someone else—regardless of what you would like to believe. Your love is also not related to whether a man falls in love with you, although that can be a great incentive. You falling in love does not occur because someone is so lovable, irresistible, or sweet. And it's not about what he does to assist you in loving him, either.

You falling in love is about you being ready, willing, and able to open your heart, emotions, spirit, and inner world to someone else, showing him you. It's about you and your readiness to love, not about him or how lovable, sweet, hot, adorable, or loving he is back.

You're hoping the feelings will rub off on you—that you'll feel a deep passionate connection because a man will, in essence, give it to you. But love doesn't work that way. You can't get it vicariously, it won't rub off on you, and no one else can give it to you.

You're holding your heart out of your relationships with men. Your heart is protected, guarded, and insulated. Very attractive people—men and women both—frequently have this dilemma because they get hit on so often, they've developed a way to protect themselves. But there is no energy or joy in being so protected, and in the end you wind up feeling empty, lonely, and disconnected from what you yearn for.

Give your heart to someone. That's the only way you're going to love.

THE MORE LOVE YOU GIVE, THE MORE "IN LOVE" YOU WILL FEEL

Dear Neil: I have gone through a series of relationships with women where I just don't feel the emotions I'd like to feel about them. Either the chemistry is wrong (and therefore I am not much into it), or she has children (I don't want children), isn't educated enough, or something else is wrong that sours me. After a while, I get dissatisfied, so I end the relationship and then find another woman—only to repeat the same scenario all over again.

In the end, I wind up not having strong emotions about any woman. I was badly hurt when I was twenty years old, and I never want to get hurt like that ever again.

I like that women fall for me. I strive to be loved by a woman—it feels so validating and confirming. I want to love again, but I can't figure out how to do it. Please help.

—Lost In Ontario

Dear Lost: Ever been with a woman who loved you passionately, who gave you everything, who was wild about you—but you didn't feel it back? That's because the passionate emotions come from giving love, not from receiving it.

Many people—especially those that did not feel very loved or valued growing up—think that to be loved in a relationship in the ultimate prize they can attain. So they focus on how to be loved or on how to get love. But they wind up feeling empty, disappointed, and cynical, because the magic feelings come much more from loving than from being loved.

You're being safe, but at a terribly high price. You're holding your heart and your emotions back so you won't get hurt again. But there is no satisfaction or joy in being so held back, and in the end you wind up being safe at the expense of being happy, passionate, and in love.

The secret that's eluding you is that you must give love in order to feel "in love." If you don't give yourself—your heart, soul, spirit, effort, and energy—you just won't feel very much, and then you'll be missing out on the emotion that many would claim is the sweetest feeling life offers.

The more love I give and the more I give of myself, the more "in love" I will feel. It's what I give to a relationship that defines how wild, how passionate, how fulfilling the experience is, not what I receive from it. (Of course, this is assuming I am not getting rejected by my partner, and where I am getting enough so that giving and receiving in the relationship are not too far out of balance.)

Challenge this stance of yours. Examine the possibility that you're being too safe—which is not at all satisfying, joyous, soulful, fun, or exhilarating.

Learn this lesson above all others: the more love I give, the more loving I feel. The more passion I offer, the more passion I generate and experience. The more I hold myself and my heart back, the emptier and more superficial the experience will feel to me.

IS THERE ANY THING I CAN DO TO BECOME A HIGHER PRIORITY?

Dear Neil: I am a sixty-nine-year-old successful, affluent businesswoman. My boyfriend of ten years is fifty-five and much less successful and affluent. He has twin daughters, age twenty-one, whom he dotes over and will do anything for. But they don't want their father to have a girlfriend.

He lives in my house and cannot afford to share all living expenses, which does not present a problem for me. But he is held in emotional hostage by the twins. He will give to them lavishly, but he has to live frugally himself. When he goes to see them, he drops me totally off his radar screen, and I lose all presence in his life. He does everything they want, when they want, with utter disregard for me, and I feel shunned and dismissed when they want something from him. Is there anything I can do about this?

—Not a Priority in Pennsylvania

Dear Not a Priority: Initiate an extremely open, honest and sober conversation with him about what each of you vision for the future of your relationship, and the quality of relationship you would like to have with each other. During the next year or two, does he see the relationship remaining about the same, or does he want it to change? What would he like to see different, and how does he envision getting from here to there? Specifically, what would he need to do in order to create that vision and what would be asked of you? Then it's your turn to address the same questions. Talk about the quality of the relationship you desire with him for the future.

Tell him that it's wonderful that he loves his daughters and is devoted to them, but that it feels awful to you because the warmth and connection between the two of you ceases, and then you feel invisible and unimportant to him. Don't make this about his daughters—that will only make him defensive. Make it about you and how you feel slighted and ignored when he's around his kids. Then tell him what behavior you'd like from him instead. Make sure to include something about the priority you'd like to hold in his life: perhaps that he can be in a warm, caring, vital relationship with you while also being a good father—and he doesn't have to ignore one while tending to the other.

It occurs to me that he may not want the relationship to get any closer—that this is as close as he may want things to get between the two of you—but is being careful because he's financially dependent on you and may fear you asking him to leave your house. It would be prudent for you to keep a watchful eye in this direction and look at how devoted and committed he actually is toward you.

In the end, you can't control what he feels about you, or what priority he assigns you in his life. But you can get clear about what it is that you need in the relationship, and you can communicate your wishes, needs, and desires, as well as what hurts, devalues, or offends you.

And you can also request different behavior—and how important that behavior is to you.

"Marriage, as far as I'm concerned, is one of the most wonderful, heartwarming, satisfying experiences a human being can have. I've only been married seventeen years, so I haven't seen that side of it yet." (George Gobel)

KEEPING YOUR RELATIONSHIP INTACT WHILE YOU'RE GOING THROUGH A CRISIS

Anytime we go through a genuine crisis, our intimate relationships with other people (your spouse or sweetheart, children, family, and friends) are affected. Whether those relationships help us through the crisis or go down in flames depends on a host of factors, most of which are within our control.

People in crisis find it difficult to socialize with others, difficult to concentrate, and difficult to have any get-up-and-go. Even small tasks or chores feel overwhelming and hard to complete. Libido diminishes considerably, and emotions other than depression or anxiety feel blunted and difficult to access. Normal things that have brought pleasure in the past—watching a movie, going out on the town, dancing, sports, sex and so on—may no longer feel pleasurable or interesting. And some people have mood spirals, where depression or anxiety keeps spiraling downward, and they get even more agitated.

A crisis strains a relationship. A person in crisis is likely to be morose, pessimistic, hopeless, sad, anxious, fatigued, and less fun to be around. People in crisis typically complain a lot. They say negative things about what's wrong with their lives, their work, their families, their partners, and with the world. They often have flat emotions, withdraw from their vital relationships, and are prone to saying or doing things that are insensitive, hostile, angry, or uncaring.

It is hard to feel loving toward someone who is giving very little back. It is hard to feel connected to someone who is withdrawn, angry, impatient, negative, or simply not present. This is profoundly multiplied if both people in a relationship are going through a crisis together, and neither of them has a whole lot to give to each other.

Here's what you can do to keep your relationship intact while one or both of you are going through a crisis:

- Affectionate touch is the one thing you can't let slide. Touch grounds us and keeps us connected to each other. Whether it's through cuddling, holding hands, hugging, or just sitting next to each other, staying in touch is vital to keeping a relationship connected through hard times. It's also wonderfully comforting to be held.

- Develop good control over your words and actions toward others. Don't take your anger or irritation out on your intimate partner, your children, or other people. It will not help you; you'll only succeed in pushing other people away.

- Make yourself go out and play together occasionally. As counterintuitive as it sounds, play and having fun reduces despair and reminds us that we're still alive. It also keeps us connected, communicating that someone is here with us through the hard times.

- Buy yourselves something you've been wanting and would enjoy.
- Create a list of goals and interests you wish to experience, achieve, accomplish, or try together.
- Dress up occasionally. Put something on that makes you feel good.
- Take turns asking each other questions, and listen to the answers: What losses are you grieving? What are you depressed about? What are you anxious about? How angry are you? How do you envision reducing these emotions so you can feel better? What helps you stay emotionally connected? How would you like me to nurture or take care of you?
- Get out in the sunlight as much as possible. If you must be indoors, sit near a window and use full-spectrum light bulbs.
- Be physically active. Motion aids emotion.
- Look beyond your current feelings. Tell yourself, "I'm more than these emotions, more than this setback or loss. I'm not going to let these things define me, ruin my life, or destroy my relationship."
- Spend time with a pet.
- Try the following communication exercise with each other, inspired by author Nathaniel Branden in his book: *If You Could Hear What I Cannot Say*. Take turns answering these questions, and answer each question thoroughly:

  I feel most connected with you when … ; You could help me to talk about my feelings more if you would … ; If I were more willing to expose how vulnerable I feel … ;

If I brought 5 percent more friendliness to my encounters with you ... ; If I were 5 percent more open to hearing your feelings ... ; If I were 5 percent more responsive to your needs ... ;

When I get withdrawn, you could pull me back by ... ; I love that you ... ; I love that we ...

- See if you can find a greater meaning in your loss.
- Eliminate sugar, caffeine, junk food and limit your intake of alcohol. You want to get through this, not numb it so that it stays buried just below the surface.
- Get help from a psychotherapist and/or a marriage and family therapist. Grieving, depression, and anxiety are all highly treatable.
- Tell your partner what you like about him/her, love about him/her, admire or respect about him/her, and cherish about him/her.

"Will you still need me, will you still feed me, when I'm sixty-four?"
(John Lennon and Paul McCartney)

REBUILDING TRUST AFTER AN AFFAIR

Dear Neil: Could you address how to rebuild trust after an affair?
—Reader From New Zealand

Dear New Zealand: What we actually mean when we say "I need to be able to trust you again" is really "I need to feel safe around you again." So rebuilding trust is akin to restoring the feeling that you're honorable, honest, truthful, trustworthy, and safe.

The other relationship has to be completely over. No repair work is going to happen if your spouse/intimate partner is not confident that the affair has stopped. This is particularly challenging when the other person is someone you regularly see at work. But if you're going to make your spouse feel safe, you will have to do whatever s/he needs. This includes you honestly confessing, telling the whole story with as much detail as your partner asks for.

Second, sincerely apologize. A sincere apology is not simply saying "I'm sorry." A sincere apology acknowledges wrongdoing, accepts accountability for the behavior, conveys genuine sorrow that you have hurt the person you love—and communicates that you will go to the end of the Earth in order to make things up to him or her. You must include an inviolable promise that you will be honest, transparent, and open about your dealings with other people from here on out and that you will never keep a hurtful secret from your partner again.

Third, you must take the lead and offer consistent effort over time to assist the relationship in being closer, friendlier, more engaged, and more deeply connected. Fourth, show your interest by being way more affectionate. Holding hands, hugging, cuddling, kissing, having your arms around each other as you watch a movie—those are ways to be affectionate through touch.

Fifth, several times a week, tell your partner what you love, admire, respect, and like about him/her. Your partner's confidence is shaken, and I cannot overstate the importance of offering a ton of reassurance—often. Sixth, be emotionally and physically available, and compassionately listen to your partner's hurt and pain. This may take a while, and you may hear the same "I can't believe this" refrain many, many times before it diminishes. Be understanding and patient. It will lessen over time.

Seventh, offer complete openness and transparency about phone records, texts, emails, credit card statements, and bills. It will give your partner assurance that you are no longer keeping secrets or being private about your dealings with other people.

Lastly, don't cheat again. Trust is way harder to regain if this happens more than once.

"Love is the irresistible desire to be desired irresistibly."
(Louis Ginsberg)

HOW IT MIGHT BE POSSIBLE TO WIN BACK TRUST

Dear Neil: My fiancé has cheated on me our entire three-year relationship, having been faithful for perhaps two months in that three-year period. He proposed to me a year ago, and has admitted that he only gave me a ring because of all the trouble he was in with me. But he hasn't been faithful since then, either.

Because of all the years of lies and deceit, I find it next to impossible to trust him. Now he wants me to trust the "new him." Can you advise me on where to start in order to regain trust for him?

—Not Sure How To Do This in Charlotte, North Carolina

Dear Charlotte: I will tell you how it might be possible for you to begin to trust him again, but first I would like to caution you that your fiancé does not sound even remotely ready to marry you, and I think it is not in your self-interest to be engaged to him at this time.

Proposing to a woman implies that a man is ready, able, prepared, and wanting to be married to her. It is not wise to propose to a woman as a way of apologizing for bad behavior, because then the woman is not going to trust that it's a serious proposal and that the man really wants to marry her. By accepting his proposal, you essentially let him off the hook for all of his previous infidelity, in essence saying that you will forgive previous indiscretions if he shapes up from now on.

But he hasn't shaped up. Since past behavior is the best predictor of future behavior, it sounds like you're unlikely to trust him no matter what he says or does, because he has violated trust too often over time. Further, we have no real reason to believe that the "new him" is anything more than a tactic or strategy designed to get you to trust him because he hasn't been able to earn it through his own trustworthy behavior.

It sounds like this man is not ready to be in a committed relationship, and that you will be destined to feel let down or broken hearted by him if you don't wake up and smell the coffee.

That being said, here's how it might be possible for him to regain your trust—if he were to do it 100 percent of the time, with no screw-ups, no lies, no deceptions, and no exceptions. But I warn you, this solution is stark, and he is unlikely to agree to this and live by this code—and therefore I am suggesting he is not ready to be engaged to you.

The solution is for him to adopt complete disclosure toward you with total transparency. He would need to give you the pass codes to all his electronic devices, including his phone and computer, social media networks, his day timer or electronic daily calendar—with every change to his schedule religiously noted before it occurs—where you would be able to phone and check out the truthfulness of everything he says he is doing and everyone he says he is doing it with.

Furthermore, he would offer you access to all of his phone contacts, including the phone numbers to all of his friends and former lovers, especially all the women with whom he cheated on you, as well as his phone bills and a history of all his text messages. You would, at your discretion, be able to call or email any of those people anytime you wanted, just to verify that he has told you the truth, the entire truth, and nothing but the truth—all the time.

This means that no secrets at all are to be kept between the two of you. Do you think he can do that? If so, he may be able to earn your trust back, because that is why someone would do all of this. But if he isn't willing to do this—all of this—my advice to you is to dump him and to go find yourself someone who can actually be yours.

"Even the wisest men make fools of themselves about women, and even the most foolish women are wise about men." (Theodor Reik)

THE PSYCHOLOGICAL MARRIAGE— AND THE PSYCHOLOGICAL DIVORCE

Dear Neil: I'm married, but I'm not in an intimate relationship, and I'm not happily married, either. We lead almost entirely separate lives, and we sleep in separate bedrooms. I am not at all confident that she loves me; she certainly doesn't act like she likes or loves me. We are married in name, but not in spirit. Is there anything I can do to change this problem? We are evangelical Christians, and we don't believe in divorce.
—Unhappy in Florida

Dear Unhappy: In every marriage there are actually three separate marriages: The marriage of the church (married in the eyes of God), the marriage of the state (your marriage certificate, which makes it legal in the eyes of the law) and the psychological marriage. For many people, the three marriages are not aligned. Some people psychologically marry way before they actually get legally married, and other people may psychologically divorce even though they remain married in the eyes of the church and the law.

Of the three marriages, you determine which one is the most significant and valuable to you. People who remain married because they think that their marriage has been blessed by God tend to stay together—whether they love each other (and enjoy each other's company) or not. People who stay together because their marriage has been sanctioned by the law are, on the whole, less committed to remain together when the going gets really tough. People who are psychologically married will fight with everything they've got to preserve the relationship and to avoid a divorce. They tend to feel more intense and more passionate toward each other than either of the others.

If all three of these marital states are aligned and connected, you are likely to be a very stable couple. But what happens when they're not aligned? What happens, for instance, when one person acts as if they've psychologically divorced the other, but they in fact remain married—which is what you've described.

So let me state the obvious: If one person psychologically divorces the other, the most important and most vital marriage is essentially over, even if you stay together. That means you might stay bonded in the eyes of God and the law, but your relationship ceases to be close and compelling, and the two of you will grow more distant, less affectionate, and less intimate.

If you are psychologically married, but you're not confident your spouse is, make a serious attempt at addressing what has happened. Ask her what distanced her from you, and what she would need in order to consider coming back to you. Ask her: "Are you getting your needs met in this relationship? If not, what would you like different?" and "What could I do—or stop doing—that would make this relationship considerately better for you than it is now?" You have to be willing to listen to her answers without anger, defensiveness, or any retaliatory comebacks. Your goal is to understand what she is feeling and what she would like different, not to defend yourself or justify your actions.

Are her requests things that you might be willing to do? If so, you increase the chances that the two of you will be able to rekindle the relationship. However, if she has no serious requests of substance, your relationship may have crossed the point of no return where it is unlikely to be resuscitated no matter what you do.

See if you can assist your relationship in warming up, by also doing such things as inviting her out on a date, holding hands, hugging, saying "I love you," leaving her sweet messages, and being kind and considerate toward her. If none of this works, are you prepared to spend the rest of your life married but psychologically divorced?

"Most people get married believing a myth—that marriage is a beautiful box full of all the things they have longed for: companionship, sexual fulfillment, intimacy, friendship. The truth is that marriage, at the start, is an empty box. You must put something in before you can take anything out. There is no love in marriage; love is in people, and people put it into marriage. There is no romance in marriage; people have to infuse it into their marriages. A couple must learn the art and form the habit of giving, loving, serving, praising—keeping the box full. If you take out more than you put in, the box will empty."
(J. Allen Peterson)

SEVEN DEADLY RELATIONSHIP SINS

Here is a list of seven deadly relationship sins:

1. **Being too detached, withdrawn, removed, guarded, or disengaged.** Not talking or not revealing your feelings. Not asking about your partner's feelings—or not taking an interest in those feelings once they are shared. Not making your relationship a top priority. Not going all out and giving your very best to the relationship. Keeping one foot out the door. Holding back. Allowing yourself to get jaded and cynical, and therefore not believing in the dream anymore. Hating men. Not trusting women. Being walled off, not sharing your inner self/emotions/hopes/dreams/ disappointments with your partner. Not letting your partner in.

2. **Being self-absorbed.** Selfish. Only looking out for yourself. Not recognizing or being tuned in to your partner's feelings. Having poor empathy for your partner's emotions, needs, desires or requests. Lack of compassion.

3. **Being defensive,** and therefore not allowing someone else to tell you what upsets, irritates, hurts or angers them. Being so self-protective that your partner doesn't feel a sense of permission or receptivity from you in order to identify what s/he thinks, feels or wants. When you can't be "wrong," you can't be in a healthy intimate relationship.

4. **Being too volatile.** Losing your temper. Saying mean things in anger that you can never truly retract. Angry outbursts, especially those that devalue your partner, or make him/her feel put down or belittled. Threatening to end the relationship if you don't get your way. Using anger in order to get your way or in order to stop a discussion.

5. **Running from a deeper connection or a greater commitment.** Being ambivalent, and therefore unsure of whether you want a relationship with the person you are with. Not matching your words of love with your behaviors.

6. **Not making important to you what's important to me.** Not being willing to blend your ways with mine, your preferences with mine, your interests with mine. Not being easily adaptable. Not being willing to honor what I want and value—or to value what's important to me.

7. **Lack of inclusion and teamwork.** Not treating me as if I'm on your side. Viewing our relationship as two adversaries rather than us being on the same team. I'll look out for me and you look out for you, rather than us looking out for each other and what's best for our relationship. Having monocular rather than binocular vision.

This is by no means an exhaustive list of relationship miscues. There are more deadly relationship sins—infidelity, dishonesty, deception, and trust issues instantly come to mind. But all of these are sins you'd be wise to get under control. If you don't, your relationships with others will be tortured—or they will cease to work at all.

"My toughest fight was with my first wife." (Muhammad Ali)

NOT TILL DEATH DO US PART:

Our Attitudes about Marriage are Changing

Our cultural attitudes about marriage, living together without getting married, and having children have been shifting dramatically. Look at these rather amazing findings about the world we are now living in.

As recently reported in the *New York Times* by David Brooks, in 1957, 57 percent of those surveyed said that they believed adults were "immoral" or "neurotic" if they remained single. Today, 45 percent of all households consist of single adults, according to the 2008 census. In 1990, almost two-thirds of Americans said that children were very important to a successful marriage. Today, only 41 percent say that. There are now more houses that have dogs than have children.

A generation or two ago, it was considered shameful for adults to have children unless they were married. Today, more than half of all births born to women under thirty occur outside of marriage. There are now more households that consist of single adults than there are married-with-children households. In Manhattan, roughly half of all residences are single households. In Denver,

Washington DC, and Atlanta, more than 40 percent of residential units are single households.

In the late 1960s, 10 percent of couples lived together before marriage. Today, 60 percent of couples live together first, and an increasing number of couples are living together and choosing not to get married. The age in which people first marry has now hit record highs: 28.7 years for men, and 26.5 for women. The divorce rate today for people fifty to sixty-four has doubled since 1990, and tripled for those sixty-five and over.

And just in case you thought this was strictly an American phenomenon, 30 percent of German women of child-bearing age say they do not intend to have children. The number of marriages in Spain has declined by 37 percent from 1975 to today. In a 2011 survey of Taiwanese women, a majority of women of child-bearing age said that they did not want children. Fertility rates in Brazil have dropped from 4.3 babies per woman to 1.9 babies in the last thirty-five years. And of course there is now same-sex marriage, which has been legalized in all or parts of the Netherlands, Belgium, Spain, Canada, South Africa, Norway, Sweden, Portugal, Iceland, Argentina, Denmark, France, England, New Zealand, Mexico, and the US—twenty-one countries as of the publication date of this book.

It is clear that attitudes are changing rapidly about marriage and the rules that govern intimate relationships, and they're changing throughout much of the world. In attempting to interpret this data, let me offer a few observations. First, people are increasingly less tolerant and less willing to remain in unsatisfactory or unhappy marriages, and today people tend to be more enlightened about what a good marriage is. Fewer and fewer people are willing to feel trapped in an unhappy relationship indefinitely.

Second, societal and religious "moral" codes of "right vs. wrong" behavior have become less honored by an increasing number of people, spanning a variety of different cultures and religions. Third, there is an increasing interest in alternative lifestyle choices, and a far greater willingness to live outside of traditional norms.

Fourth, there is an unmistakable acknowledgement that marriage is hard to successfully traverse over a long period of time. (In 2011, several lawmakers in Mexico City proposed the creation of renewable marriage contracts, where you would in essence get married for a couple of years, and then you would have the option of renewing the contract or opting out. The law was not passed, but the fact that it was proposed in Mexico, an overwhelmingly Catholic country, tells us that people are seriously reconsidering the wisdom of the marriage contract as we have always known it.)

The vows that we take, "Till death do us part," come from the middle ages, where the average life span was thirty years of age. Today the average life span is approximately eighty for women and seventy-five for men. (In New Zealand, it is seventy-eight for men and eighty-two for women. In Japan, it is seventy-nine for men and eighty-six for women.) So now, when you're forty and you're looking at the face across the breakfast table, you can pause and ask: "Another forty years of you? Another forty years of this?"

You can see why "Till death do us part" didn't have the same meaning that it does today, and it's a much bigger challenge than it used to be.

That being said, when a marriage works today, it works better than it has ever worked in the past. There is more communication, more shared decision making, more equality, more respect, less violence, more closeness, and greater connection for an ever larger number of couples spanning different cultures and continents, and encompassing an ever wider range of lifestyle choices.

"Before marriage, a man will lay awake all night thinking about something you said; after marriage, he'll fall asleep before you finish saying it." (Helen Rowland)

MONEY ARGUMENTS REVEAL POWERFUL UNDERLYING ISSUES

Dear Neil: We have been fighting about money issues for years. We argued about money when we were doing very well, and we're fighting about money now, when we're not. We disagree on how money is to be spent, what our financial priorities are, how to handle it when we disagree about a purchase, and how much credit card debt we should carry. Right now this is complicated by us earning less than half the income we were making two years ago. Why is money such a hot-button issue for us? We know we're not the only people having to get by on less.

—Arguing in Washington

Dear Arguing: There's a good chance that you're actually fighting about underlying subterranean issues that often drive our emotions on this subject. Here are some of the most common hidden issues related to money:

- **Power and control:** Are each person's needs and desires around money considered equally, or does one person have more financial power than the other? Is one person considered more important than the other because s/he earns most of the money? (If so, the other person is bound to grow resentful and angry.) Who makes the decisions about how money is spent? Are my opinions and feelings valued and listened to, or are major decisions made without me? Especially if you're someone with little or no income of your own, you may feel financially powerless—less than equal—while viewing your partner as quite powerful, which is likely to lead to you eventually withdrawing or withholding yourself emotionally, sexually, or in some other way. Power imbalances over money tend to injure intimacy and closeness over time. If you want to reduce or eliminate this issue, make sure both of you feel you have more or less equal say about how joint money is to be spent, saved, or invested, and what financial freedoms each person has.

- **Acknowledgement/Recognition:** Sometimes the unaddressed or unrecognized issue has to do with not being acknowledged or appreciated for what you contribute to the relationship. Whether your contribution is primarily a paycheck, supplemental income, sex, pregnancy and child care, household chores, cooking meals, or of being the emotional lifeline of the household—if someone feels unacknowledged, undervalued, unappreciated, or taken for granted, s/he will inevitably feel hurt, resentful, and angry—which will lead to greater distance between the two of you. One way of getting even or of expressing anger and resentment is to violate an agreement about how money is used—and what it's used for. If you wish to defeat this issue, call attention on a regular basis to what your intimate partner brings to the relationship, how s/he increases your happiness and well-being, and how his/her contribution to the relationship is vital, valued, and appreciated.

- **Trust:** Can I trust you to do the right thing concerning our money? Can I trust that we will make important financial decisions together (so that our relationship feels like a partnership instead of two separate individuals)? Can I trust you to not take advantage of me financially? Can I trust you to act honorably and honestly, and to tell me the whole truth as it relates to money and our finances?
- **How important am I to you?** If I see you valuing your own needs or honoring someone else's desires more than you value my needs and desires, I will not feel cared for by you, as if my feelings or wishes are just not that important to you. Defeating this issue requires that you act in ways that demonstrate that you are paying attention to and respecting my needs, my happiness, my feelings, my desires, and my well-being.
- **Commitment:** How I trust you with my/our money is frequently a strong reflection of how strong my commitment is to you.

"What a woman tells a passionate lover should be written in wind and running water." (John Fowles)

THE BASICS OF ROMANTIC INTELLIGENCE

When we think of intelligence, we usually think of doing well in school, getting good grades and generally being the equivalent of a rocket scientist. That is called intellectual intelligence, and we refer to it as IQ (intelligence quotient). But there is also social intelligence (SQ), emotional intelligence (EQ), and romantic intelligence (RQ). All four co-mingle and work together within our lives.

Romantic intelligence is about being smart in love, and it is a far more accurate indicator of your overall level of happiness and well-being than your IQ. To be successful in love is to be successful in life. Most of us know people who have been very successful at work but whose lives we would not want ourselves.

Here are the basic requirements of romantic intelligence, taken from the book *Romantic Intelligence* by Mary and John Valentis (New Harbinger).To be smart in love you must be able to:

- Have an awareness to recognize exactly what emotions you are experiencing in the moment.

- Assess whether to act on your emotions or not. You must be able to think a problem through rather than acting impulsively, and later regretting your actions.

- Persist through adversity, never giving up on the dream, and motivating both yourself and others to bring out the best each of you have. To be an emotional leader in your relationship, taking responsibility for making your relationship deeper, more precious and meaningful.

- Push through and regulate painfully paralyzing emotions that hold you back (fear, depression, anxiety, etc.) by understanding and accepting these emotions as part of life's painful experiences but not letting them run your life.

- Eliminate sarcasm, put-downs, needless conflicts, petty squabbles, and nitpicking as a way of saving face. It is essential to work through an entire problem step by step, rather than momentarily feeling better about yourself by winning a battle at the expense of wrecking your relationship.

- Know how and when to express anger assertively—not aggressively—and to also know when not to express anger at all. You must learn to build up your tolerance for frustration and sometimes delay gratification.

- Become proficient at empathy/listening, which means you have the ability to put aside your own thoughts, feelings, and needs for the moment; being an open channel and tuning into other people's emotional states (as well as your own); being able to follow someone else's emotional lead; being able to listen attentively to what your partner is saying rather than thinking about what you are going to say next, and being able to listen without interrupting your partner.

- Develop and keep emotional self-control over intense negative emotions so that they serve as a signal for solving difficult issues. It does not help to direct negativity at your partner, which will hurt—and ultimately destroy—your relationship.

- Be sensitive to your partner's emotional states, which will allow you to solve problems between the two of you with greater compassion. Strive to understand more of what your partner wants and needs from you. Adopt an altruistic attitude and strive to be aware of what your partner is feeling about him/herself.

"Only two things are necessary to keep one's wife happy. One is to let her think she is having her own way, and the other, to let her have it." (Lyndon B. Johnson)

QUIZ: HOW EMPATHETIC ARE YOU?

Empathy is the ability to feel the emotions of someone else. It describes how well we identify with other people's pain, fears, desires, feelings, and experiences. It is the trait that most emotionally connects two human beings together. It makes me have compassion for what has befallen you, it allows you to feel excited by my success, and it compels both of us to be horrified when we hear or read about some tragedy that has befallen others.

To test your level of empathy, take the following quiz. Use this scale for all questions: A. Not at all. B. Somewhat. C. Fifty-fifty. D. A good deal. E. Very much.

1. I enjoy caring for other people.

2. I can usually appreciate the other person's viewpoint, even if I don't agree with it.

3. I am quick to spot when someone else is feeling awkward or uncomfortable.

4. People tell me that I often go too far in driving home my point in a discussion.

5. I am easily affected by the emotions of others.
6. I find it easy to put myself in someone else's shoes.
7. I can tell if someone is masking their true emotions.
8. I am able to make decisions without being influenced by feelings of people close to me.
9. Friends usually confide in me about their troubles or problems.
10. It upsets me if I hear of an animal being mistreated or if I see an animal in pain.
11. I find myself having the same emotions as the characters in the movies I see or in the books I read.
12. Sometimes I don't understand why some people get offended by a remark or a comment that I make.
13. When I talk with people, we tend to talk about their feelings or experiences rather than mine.
14. I am a natural-born counselor.
15. I get angry over injustice.
16. Other people have said that I was insensitive, even though I don't exactly understand why.

Scoring: To tally your score, for numbers 1, 2, 3, 5, 6, 7, 9, 10, 11, 13, 14 and 15, give yourself 0 points. For numbers 4, 8, 12 and 16, give yourself 4 points for each "A" answer, 3 points for every "B" answer, 2 points for every "C" response, 1 point for every "D" answer, and 0 points for each "E" answer.

If you total 0—24 points, you have low levels of empathy. You tend toward being cool, even distant. You find it difficult to relate to the feelings of others or to identify with their pain or their struggles.

If you total 25—40 points, you have average levels of empathy. You can understand how other people are feeling, at least some of the time, even though you may not always get it right the first time. If you total over 40 points, you have higher levels of empathy. You are easily able to pick up the emotional cues of other people's emotions, and you are likely very bonded to an animal as well.

Empathy can increase with the desire to be more attuned to other people and other living things. It requires that you pay close attention to how things would feel if they happened to you. It allows you to temporarily step into someone else's shoes, so to speak, in order to fully understand why they feel as they do, and why they act as they do.

"The price is exorbitant, the pleasure is transitory and the position is ridiculous." (Lord Chesterfield on sex)

HOW TO RUIN YOUR RELATIONSHIP

The variety of couples in the news who are separating or divorcing is a sober reminder that our intimate relationships are fragile and can break—and that they must be handled with proper care and maintenance.

Many things can go wrong in a marriage. But there are things you can do—or stop doing—that directly relate to the health, well-being, and longevity of your relationship. I will describe what behaviors destroy a relationship, and several chapters from now I will address what you can do to strengthen your relationship so you stand a better chance of living in greater peace and harmony with each other.

Here are some of the more common ways people destroy their intimate relationship:

- Being walled off and hard to reach. Being emotionally or physically distant, closed or withholding. A variation of this is to stonewall your intimate partner, which means that rather than addressing what bothers you, you wall off, and s/he has to guess what's upsetting you or what you want.

- Poor listening skills. Most people talk way more than they listen, and they don't listen to genuinely understand.

- Not making important to you that which is important to your partner. This includes not blending your ways, your preferences, or your interests with his or hers and not being adaptable to someone else. It also means not being willing to honor your partner's wants, needs, or desires.

- Not making your intimate relationship your top priority. It's easy to treat work, children, family, friends, sports, computer, or TV as urgent and critical. Do that, and your partner will not feel s/he matters to you.

- Reduced affection. Hand-holding, hugs, cuddling, and physical tenderness are a glue that keeps two people close and connected to each other. If affection is low, your relationship has likely grown distant.

- Not being communicative. It is essential to communicate your needs, wants, desires, and dreams to your partner. To not do so forces your partner to be a mind-reader, and absolutely nobody is a good mind-reader.

- Being critical, argumentative, rebellious, or rude. It makes you difficult to be around, and it's embarrassing and annoying.

- Being defensive and therefore not allowing someone else to tell you what upsets, irritates, hurts, or angers them. Over time, your mate learns to not say things that will cause you to react, and that will shut down communication, connection, and closeness. Act defensive and watch your relationship grow more brittle and distant.

- Low trust. It's very hard to be with someone who is chronically suspicious, jealous, or mistrusting—or who has a hard time giving you the benefit of doubt.

- Seeking stimulation in all the wrong places—using alcohol, drugs, shopping, eating, porn, work, an affair, or any number of other escapes. It separates and distances the two of you from each other.

- Control. If you're controlling in a relationship, you're predictably creating a power struggle that you're unlikely to win. No one wants to be controlled or to feel powerless, so shared decision making is the wisest way to go.

- Dishonesty. It's impossible to trust someone who doesn't act trustworthy. Anyone who is secretive, hidden, withholding of important personal information—or who has deceived, misled, or betrayed you in the past—is extremely hard to trust. And low trust is the death knell for most relationships, because once trust is broken, there will always be a seed of mistrust that remains.

- Not taking accountability for your words, actions, or behaviors—or feeling so self-justified that you seldom think you owe an apology for your hurtful, insensitive, or demeaning words or behaviors.

- Having an anger issue or being resentful, sarcastic, or passive-aggressive. Your partner will either avoid you or will become afraid of you. Either one will destroy closeness, connection, and trust. Being angry is not an acceptable reason for wounding another person or treating him/her disrespectfully—ever.

- Acting narcissistic, self-absorbed, or self-centered. Looking out for you, not for the welfare or the happiness of your partner—or your relationship.
- Disinterest in sex, or sexual rejection. Your partner will inevitably feel resentful, rejected, and angry.
- Infidelity. The best method ever for starting a nuclear war.

"Any married man should forget his mistakes–no use two people remembering the same thing." (Duane Dewel)

THE WAY TO LOSE DEFENSIVENESS

Suppose your intimate partner said something that hurt your feelings, and you retaliate with a cutting remark. You are angry, and you try to think of the reasons why s/he was so hurtful to you. So you come up with a story about her that justifies your behavior and your anger. "She's so insensitive to my feelings." "No matter what I do for her, it's never enough." "If she really loved me, she wouldn't talk that way to me."

These thoughts are your "answer" to what happened; they are what your mind manufactures in the service of your righteous anger. In fact, these thoughts about her further intensify your emotions, causing you to distance yourself even more from the love you feel for her.

Instead of justifying your feelings with your thoughts, try staying with your feelings by asking yourself, "What's inside me that's making me angry right now?" or "What's going on that's making me hurt right now?" You can substitute any other emotion in this question and arrive at what your feeling is trying to communicate to you.

Usually you will discover that your intense reaction is due to something greater than the current disagreement you're are having with your partner. For instance, when somebody important in your past disapproved of or criticized you, you may have felt "bad" or unlovable. Your intimate partner's critical message and tone of voice may have reignited your emotions from the past.

Now suppose you discover that when you are criticized, you feel shame and embarrassment, because deep down within yourself you believe that any criticism must mean that there is something really wrong with you—so wrong that you are unlovable and can't ever be loved.

If you can't be loved, then eventually your life partner will tire of you and dump you. When you make that connection, you then see that the issue is really your fear of abandonment—which you have associated with your partner's criticism.

If you choose to share this insight with your partner, you will lose your defensiveness. Such emotional honesty will draw you closer together because your openness about such a painful subject will create a deeper intimacy between the two of you.

One other tool will help you to be less defensive and more emotionally intelligent is nondefensive, empathetic listening. Such listening takes place when you defer your own needs for a while to concentrate your attention on your partner while s/he is speaking.

Hearing becomes listening only when you give your full attention to what is being said and how it is said. When you really listen, you are certainly not thinking about what you are going to say next or how you will respond.

You show that you're listening to your partner by paraphrasing his or her words, making eye contact, nodding your head attentively, leaning toward your partner, and not interrupting. You make your partner feel visible, when s/he speaks to you about something important, and you give your undivided attention. You can even let him/her know you understand by using such romantically intelligent phrases as "I can understand how you can see it like that," or "Your feelings make sense."

This is one of the biggest keys to being more romantically intelligent.

Source: *Romantic Intelligence* by Mary and John Valentis (New Harbinger).

"My wife ran off with my best friend, and I miss him." (Anonymous)

EROTIC TALK ADDS SPICE TO YOUR RELATIONSHIP

Erotic talk, called "verbal foreplay" by Bonnie Gabriel (www.lovetalk.org) in the book *The Fine Art Of Erotic Talk* (Bantam Books) is about talking in sensuous ways that generate passion between you and your lover.

Here are some Gabriel suggestions about how you can add erotic talk to spice up your intimate relationship:

Learn the art of "erotic subtext." If you "sensualize" expressions—that is, use words that evoke a sense of physical or emotional connection to your partner—your words will become especially potent. And remember to use all of your senses. For instance, you may give your partner an honest compliment like "I love the way you dance." But you can help to create a more romantic or erotic mood with expressions like "I love the way you feel in my arms" or "I love the way you move your body."

You can express your enjoyment of how your intimate partner sounds by saying, "Your voice excites me." "Keep talking to me that way." In the visual realm, you might tell your partner "I love looking at you," " You make that dress look fabulous," "When you look at me like that, I begin to melt."

Don't forget to notice if you're attracted to your partner's scent. You might say something like "I love your perfume," or "I like your cologne," although a more sensual way of putting it would be "I love the way you smell," or "Your skin has the nicest perfume; I could breathe you in like this all night."

And if it's appropriate, remember to include your sense of taste. This sense is engaged whenever you touch your partner's skin with your lips. So why not let him or her know how much you are enjoying such contact with expressions like "I love the way your lips taste," or "Your skin tastes delicious."

You can build intimacy by validating your partner's affectionate behavior toward you. You might say "I like the way you take my hand when we walk down the street," or "It felt really nice when you stroked my hair in the movie theater." In doing so, you are not only showing your appreciation but optimizing your chances for the affectionate behavior you enjoy to be repeated.

Perfect your ability and skills in creating erotic afterglow: learn to use words to leave your lover wanting more. The secret to creating erotic afterglow for you and your lover is based on three principles. The first is to express your thanks and appreciation for all the pleasure your partner has given you. The second is to build a provocative mood of positive expectation—or even delicious suspense—of what your future sexual encounters will hold. And the third is to continue to remind your lover of the special connection you have together even when you're not together. Examples: "This is better than the book or the movie!" "That was absolutely delicious!" "If I could bottle and sell the way you make me feel, I would make a fortune." "Thank you for letting me love every inch of you." "I feel that you've pleasured every molecule of my being!"

Create previews of coming attractions. Describe some of the ways you plan to pleasure your partner the next time you are together. For instance, "The next time, I'm going to treat you to a long sensuous massage that will sensitize every nerve ending in your body," or "Next time, I am going to wear a black corset and high-heeled boots."

These exercises, when used appropriately, can be effective in all stages of courtship and marriage, as well as foreplay and sex.

"Sexual activity is only the difference between your fantasy and friction." (Helen Singer Kaplan)

THE FINE ART OF EROTIC TALK

Most men and women find that erotic words and voice tone are important ingredients in their arousal. In her book *"The Fine Art of Erotic Talk"* Bonnie Gabriel says words are wonderful aphrodisiacs. "Through words, you can stimulate the pleasure centers in your partner's mind so they send shivers of sensual delight through his entire body. Through words, you can help her become more relaxed and receptive to your touch. Through words, you can ignite his erotic imagination or lift her to the heights of unbridled passion. And through words, you can melt the barriers that may be keeping you and your lover from experiencing the profound joy of a sacred sexual union."

Interested? Close your eyes for a moment and imagine that your beloved, or someone to whom you're very attracted, is calling out your name. First imagine that there is an undertone of "you're very precious to me" in his or her voice. Notice how the uttering of your name in this context makes you feel. Now, imagine that the message your lover is conveying with the repeated calling of your name is "I want you now." Does that generate different feelings and reactions in your body?

This is an example of erotic talk, which Gabriel defines as any verbal or vocal expression that generates or intensifies passion.

To increase your skill in this area, Gabriel offers the following exercises:

- Create a sexy voice. When we hear the term "sexy" used to describe someone's voice quality, most of think of that husky, throaty, breathy sound. To get that breathy quality associated with a sexy voice, open your mouth and count out loud "81, 82, 83, 84, 85 and so on until you reach "89. Next, repeat the count from 81 to 89, only this time punctuate each count with a breath of air. Finally, alternate between the normal sound and the breathy sound. A tip: the erotic voice needs more oxygen, so remember to inhale more frequently than you normally do.
- Just switching from normal to soft volume in the middle of a conversation can be erotic. Try the sentence "Since we've both got some free time, what would you like to do tonight?" First, ask the entire question in your normal conversational tone. Then try asking the first part in your conversational tone, and drop your voice when you say "what would you like to do tonight?" Finally, try asking the entire question in a soft voice. Which sounds the most sexually inviting to you?
- Ask a provocative question with a hidden or implied message. For example: "Are you always this funny, or am I inspiring you?" "Do your eyes always light up like this, or is it my irresistible charm that is making them sparkle?"
- One of the most powerful ways to connect more deeply with your partner is to maintain eye contact and verbal connection

while you're in the midst of an erotic experience with each other. You might begin by telling your lover, "I want to see the love and desire in your eyes as I touch you like this, and I want you to see it in mine." Even if you find yourself feeling a bit uncomfortable the first few times you do this, stay with it. Eventually the discomfort will pass, and you will find yourself opening to new levels of trust, intimacy and passion.

"If I told you you have a beautiful body, you wouldn't hold it against me, would you?" (David Fisher)

WHAT TO DO IF YOU'VE GROWN APART

Dear Neil: Over the past two years my husband has been disconnecting from me. He says it's me just being emotional, but he doesn't touch/cuddle me anymore, and he is no longer interested in how I feel. I don't think that we will last much longer. Do you have any advice?
—No Longer Close in Denver

Dear Denver: See if you can engage your husband in a very open and honest discussion about the differing emotions the two of you feel about the state of your marriage. This is a discussion to explore feelings, air emotions, and to correct problems. Your goal is to speak your feelings and to hear his feelings, not to defend yourself or justify your behavior. Sit facing each other holding hands, with each of you taking turns answering each question thoroughly before you go on to the next question:

I have been protecting and/or hiding myself by …

It hurt me when …

I remain hurt about …

I'm angry about …

I distance and withdraw from you by …

Sometimes I can hurt you by …

When I am withdrawn, you could pull me back by …

I have contributed to the problems between us by …

If we were going to solve the problems in our relationship, I would need to …

If we were to solve the problems in our relationship, I would need for you to …

The most important things you could do that would help me to be closer to you are …

I would like to apologize for …

I would feel greater support from you if you would …

I would feel greater respect from you if you would …

Trust would be stronger for me if you would …

I would feel that you were putting greater effort into the relationship if you would …

I would like us to do more fun activities together, such as …

It would feel that you were being more of a team player if you would …

We could prevent harmful interactions between us if you would … If I would …

I could assist us in feeling closer and more intimate by …

You could assist me in feeling closer and more intimate by …

I would like for us to accomplish or experience sometime in the next five years …

We could make more time to meet our goals and to do the things that give us pleasure if you were to … if I were to …

I would love it if you would nurture/spoil me more by …

I would be willing to nurture/spoil you more in the ways you are requesting if …

If I knew for certain that we were going to work everything out and stay together, I would …

Please forgive me for …
I forgive you for…
I love that we are…
I love that you are…
I feel especially cherished by you when …
I feel most connected with you when …

"What do men want? Men want a mattress that cooks." (Judy Tenuta)

EMOTIONAL VIAGRA

Let's say it's been years since you and your partner have talked meaningfully about what you liked, loved, admired, respected, or found attractive about each other. If that's the case—or close to it—we can assume that, although the two of you remain together, and perhaps even still have sex, most of the warmth has left your relationship. Your relationship just doesn't feel that close anymore.

So what can you do to warm the relationship up? What needs to occur for the two of you to emotionally reconnect so you're feeling closer and more intimate with each other?

Probably, you already know the answer. Most of us know what we can say or do that would create warmth and help our partner soften toward us. I'm not talking about grand gestures, such a surprise trip somewhere or dozens of flowers but rather small, doable, nonextravagant gestures that you could make a part of your day-to-day repertoire—that may ultimately mean more.

Ellen Wachtel, who presents this idea in her book: *We Love Each Other But ...* (St. Martin's Griffin) says "When people are angry and hurt, they gradually stop doing the things that make their partner feel warmly toward them. Often this happens without any plan or conscious decision. Few of us actually decide to withhold or punish, although of course this can happen. Rather, when we feel hurt and angry it just doesn't occur to us be emotionally generous."

Here's Wachtel's suggestion: When one person breaks the cycle of withholding and acts emotionally generous, the atmosphere of tension and/or distance begins to soften. So think about it. Did your significant other like it when you left notes? Sent cards? Gave flowers? Cooked a favorite meal? When you invited her out on a date? When the two of you did more things together or as a family? When you did one of her chores unexpectedly? When you let him sleep in? When you were more romantic or seductive? When you went out of your way to gently teach or nurture a child?

You don't have to already be feeling warm to do those things that are likely to warm up your relationship. You can be feeling rather hurt or withdrawn or miffed and still do positive gestures of goodwill—with the desire to communicate that you value your partner's happiness—and that you are making daily efforts to nurture your relationship and to help the two of you to feel closer to each other.

What you are shooting for is to soften the atmosphere of tension and distance—with emotionally generous behaviors that are intended to rekindle the feelings of greater warmth and love. Your partner may not reciprocate, and certainly not immediately, but be patient and continue to reach out anyway.

You may be wondering why you should be more positive and complimentary when your partner is not. The answer is that sometimes it only takes one person to change the energy and improve the atmosphere in the relationship, and the hope is that once your partner feels more appreciated and valued, s/he will begin to warm up to you.

Think about it. What could you possibly lose by doing this?

"Love is the same as like except you feel sexier. And more romantic. And also more annoyed when he talks with his mouth full. And you also resent it more when he interrupts you. And you also respect him less when he shows any weakness. And furthermore, when you ask him to pick you up at the airport and he tells you he can't do it because he's busy, it's only when you love him that you hate him." (Judith Viorst)

QUIZ: HOW GOOD A LISTENER ARE YOU?

By far the most common complaint marriage counselors hear is the statement, "We can't communicate."

There are many reasons why communication stops or becomes superficial and brittle, including poor conflict resolution, problem solving, compromising and negotiating skills; withholding information; keeping secrets from each other; and becoming defensive—to name a few. But one of the most overlooked reasons is because many of us have poor listening skills.

How well do you listen? Take this quiz to find out. Using the following scale, rate each question with the closest number.

Scale: 1 (Virtually Never); 2 (Seldom); 3 (Sometimes); 4 (Often); 5 (Very Frequently)

1. You seem to often have trouble being able to accuratcly rccall the details about a conversation.

2. You are uncomfortable asking questions as a way of encouraging someone to open up to you. People will tell you what they want you to know, and anything else feels like prying.

3. How frequently do you get interrupted by phone calls, texts, emails, social media postings, or other distractions when you're talking with someone else?

4. In a restaurant or other public place, how frequently do you listen in on other conversations when you're engaged in your own conversation with other people?

5. How often do you finish other people's sentences for them or complete the jokes or stories they tell?

6. How often do you interrupt when you have something to say during a conversation?

7. You listen more for the facts than the feelings in attempting to understand what someone is saying to you.

8. After someone tells you a story, how likely are you to follow up with your own story?

9. People have told you that it doesn't feel like you're listening when they are talking to you.

10. You are often thinking about your response when other people are talking.

11. It's your observation that watching the other person's body language is seldom helpful in understanding what is being said. It's the words that are important, not those nonverbal cues.

12. People have said you seem spaced out a lot.

13. You find yourself interrupting another person's conversation frequently.

14. You can carry on a conversation while watching TV, checking emails, or otherwise engaged in some other task.

15. It's not that important to look at who is talking to you. You can multi-task and still listen.

16. You sometimes cut people off in midsentence in order to give your opinion or say how you feel.

17. People seldom seek you out when they need a sounding board or want to talk about a problem. This puzzles you.

18. Usually in a conversation, you're the one who talks the most.

19. You are quick to correct someone if they mispronounce a word or say something you disagree with.

Scoring: Total all your scores. If your score falls in the 19–43 range, you are a wonderful listener, and other people are likely to seek you out when they want (or need) to talk.

If your score is 44–57, you are a good conversationalist, but you could improve by focusing more on the other person, interrupting less, and making the conversation less about you and more about the other person.

If your score is 58 or above, your desire is to talk, not listen. This makes you a difficult person for someone to share their inner feelings with.

Good listening involves more than just hearing. It is an active, not a passive process, and it requires asking questions, offering comments and keeping the focus on somebody else instead of on yourself. It requires your presence and your interest. If you don't offer that, another person will sense your lack of presence and genuine concern—and will then be very likely to clam up around you.

One of the easiest ways of stopping another person from opening up to you is to cut them off midsentence because you have something important you want to say—because you will communicate that what you have to say trumps what s/he has to say.

An extremely useful technique is to summarize what the other person has said and then ask whether you understand him or her correctly. If you combine that with using words of encouragement ("I understand," "Tell me more about that," "Keep on going," "Is there more?") you will increase your listening skills dramatically.

Also, refrain from offering advice unless the other person specifically asks for your advice. And whenever you can, offer validation and empathy, which is what most of us are looking for a lot of the time.

"When I was very young, I kissed my first woman and smoked my first cigarette on the same day. Believe me, never since have I wasted any more time on tobacco." (Arturo Toscanini)

QUIZ: ARE YOU CONTROLLING?

Do you think you are controlling? Do other people tell you that you are too controlling? Do your relationships have a history of control issues or power struggles? Have lovers and/or spouses objected to you making important decisions without them? Take this quiz to gauge how controlling you are.

Answer the following questions using this scale. 1 = rarely or never; 2 =seldom; 3 = sometimes; 4 = often; 5 = very often.

1. Do you react negatively or defensively when someone offers you constructive criticism or makes a request of you to do something different?

2. Do you feel uncomfortable when someone gets too close to you emotionally? Do you push away when things are close?

3. Are you a "back-seat" driver?

4. Are you the one who has to drive virtually all the time?

5. In stressful situations or when things don't go according to plan, are you quick to anger or become irritable?

6. Do you find it difficult to trust other people?
7. In a relationship, do you get your way most of the time? Are things done your way most of the time?
8. In a relationship, do you want to know where your intimate partner is at all times?
9. In a relationship, are you prone to jealousy?
10. Are you a perfectionist, or do you set very high standards for yourself?
11. Because of your high standards, do other people feel criticized by you?
12. Do other people feel they can't measure up to your standards or expectations?
13. Do you feel vulnerable and out of sorts when you have to depend on other people?
14. Do you dominate discussions? Are you the "take charge" type?
15. Do you get people to do things for you?
16. Do you find it difficult to effectively work as a team?
17. Are you your own worst critic?
18. Do you interrupt people a lot?
19. In your personal life, do you give other people advice or direction way more than they give you advice or direction?
20. Are you a very organized person?

21. Are you typically the center of attention?
22. In a relationship when you're in a fight, do you tend to win most of the time?
23. Do you take charge of the money in your household and demand explanations for expenditures you haven't agreed to?
24. Do you react negatively or defensively when someone challenges you or your choices?
25. In a relationship, do you make important decisions without first getting the agreement of your significant other?

Scoring:

If your combined score is 88–125, you are controlling of other people. You likely elicit resentment, anger and withdrawal from other people.

If your combined score is 70–87, you have your moments of being controlling, but you're not usually considered a "control freak." You may wish to examine your insecurities more deliberately.

If your combined score is 55–69, you may value being in control over yourself, but not normally over other people.

If your combined score is 54 or below, you are not considered controlling.

"I've never won an argument with my wife; and the only time I thought I had, I had found out the argument wasn't over yet." (Jimmy Carter)

BECOMING AN EMOTIONALLY AVAILABLE PERSON

Dear Neil: I can understand your recommendation to avoid emotionally unavailable people like myself who have these deep personal flaws. But not one of us who are damaged people want to be where we are. From lousy childhoods to a series of failed relationships, our lack of progress about becoming emotionally more available is quite depressing.

Let's assume your message is taken to heart by the mentally and spiritually unblemished. What about the rest of us? Many of us lack the resources on multiple levels to become the beautiful souls that professional therapy might promise. In the future, would you please offer those of us on the other side of the relationship tracks some words that will help us grow toward having a happy relationship?

—Despondent in Colorado

Dear Despondent: Deep down, if I feel inadequate and fear that I don't measure up, then sooner or later I'm going to be afraid that you'll find out about me, agree that I'm not good enough, and eventually dump me. So if I remain distant from you, aloof, and disengaged, and I don't give you a whole lot of my time, it won't hurt as much when you tell me you're going to leave me. I have retreated into a web of self-protection and safety so I won't get too hurt when things don't work out, because deep down I don't feel I deserve to be loved.

Such half-hearted attempts at love will keep me safe, but they will sabotage my ability to create a connected, loving and trusting relationship. How close am I going to allow myself to be when I'm secretly trying to be less emotionally invested because I fear you're going to reject me?

I am also insecure and have low self-esteem. That means I get threatened and/or jealous easily, and I'll get defensive or angry if I feel you're putting me down, criticizing me, telling me I'm inadequate in some way, or being disrespectful toward me. This means you can't actually tell me what you think or feel if it goes against what I want to hear, because if you do, I will make it very emotionally costly for you. And I feel empty enough that most of the time, I'm needing to tend to my own needs, interests, and desires, and I may not be able to devote time and effort to your desires and needs.

This description is at the heart of why I am emotionally unavailable. You can see I have a lot of battles I'm fighting, and why I might not be there for you the way you want me to be.

If I were going to become a more emotionally available person, here's what I will need to do:

First, I have to examine my feelings of not feeling worthy of a close, loving relationship. I would have to challenge my assumption that if you really get to know me, you will eventually reject me, and I would have to discover and embrace why I am lovable and why I am deserving of your love.

Second, I would have to tune into your feelings and needs and be very careful that I don't place my needs and wants above yours.

I would need to develop a greater level of empathy and compassion for your feelings, desires, needs, and requests.

Third, I would have to act trustworthy, accountable, and responsible. I could not afford to permit myself to have a secret life or someone else on the side, and I would have to offer you complete transparency (access to my computer, phone, text records, and so on) in order to clean up any trust issues that I generated in the past. I would have to keep no secrets at all from you.

Forth, I would have to make time for you. I would have to treat you (and our kids) as top priorities in my life, and I would make myself assessable and available to you the vast majority of the time.

Fifth, I would have to cease being volatile, losing my temper, acting mean-spirited, or saying hurtful things to you. I would never again threaten to end the relationship if I didn't get my way or use anger in order to get my way.

Sixth, I would commit to letting you in, by sharing my inner dreams, hopes, fears, disappointments, and emotions with you. I would quit walling my inner self off from you and allow myself to be known—warts and all.

Finally, I would become a better listener, gain control over my addictions, commit to being more of a giver than a taker, and cease being so judgmental and critical of you—and of myself.

"Love is a fire. But whether it is going to warm your hearth or burn down your house, you can never tell." (Joan Crawford)

PERIODIC REPAIR WORK IS REQUIRED IN A RELATIONSHIP

Oftentimes, people fight about next to nothing. Take, for instance, the following example of a couple trying to decide which restaurant to go to. She says: "Let's eat Chinese food tonight." He says: "I'd prefer pizza." She says: "We always eat pizza; let's try something else." He says: "Pizza is what I like. I don't want something else." She says: "You're so inflexible and boring, and you always want the same thing." He says: "I'm going to get pizza. Are you coming, or are we eating separately tonight?" She says: "I hope you choke on your pizza," and walks out of the room.

So what were they fighting about?

Perhaps they were fighting about nothing more significant than momentary irritation. But a healthy couple finds a way to do some repair work on the incident soon thereafter, something like: Her: "I'm sorry for saying you should choke on your pizza. I didn't mean that. Please forgive me." Him, responding: "Perhaps I'm getting too set in my ways. Why don't you choose the next place for us to eat, and I'll go along with whatever you choose. I get that you want a more varied menu than I do, and I'll be more responsive to that in the future."

But let's say they don't do that repair work, as many couples don't. The incident, which by itself may not have been important, is now left to grow and fester. Pretty soon, it's not just a regrettable momentary irritation, but a larger issue. She now says that he isn't responsive to her wishes, that he doesn't treat her with respect, that he's controlling and unable to blend in a long-term relationship.

Now the couple has a real problem. The minor incident, not repaired, has now grown into a possible relationship-threatening issue. But if the couple didn't repair the original incident, they are likely to be ill-equipped and unskilled in knowing how to address and resolve the larger and more emotional issues they now face.

There are three common ways that get otherwise committed relationships into trouble. First, is by not addressing the important issues when they first arise, thereby allowing hurt emotions to grow and fester. Second, is by not revisiting the hurtful words or behaviors shortly after they occur—and to do the repair work so that small incidents do not mushroom into bigger issues.

Finally, many people get way too emotional when challenged with an important issue or hurt feelings and therefore respond with anger or rage, sarcasm, name-calling, harsh judgements, criticism, threats—in short, too much raw emotion or defensiveness—which poisons the whole environment between them and discourages people from talking openly and honestly with each other.

Here is the better way: first, lay the disagreements and conflicts out on the table, so problems can be addressed and resolved in a civil and constructive way. It's important that the two of you are respectful of each other—no exceptions.

Second, make sure you do periodic repair work by apologizing for wrongdoing or words that hurt or behaviors that offend. This repair work is not just desirable—it's required if you have an interest in staying together and being reasonably happy with each other.

Third, you cannot respond with anger, aggression, threats, or defensiveness if your partner tells you that something you said or did—or didn't say or didn't do—has hurt, angered, or offended them. Your partner has to tell you what's bothering him or her; that's how repair work happens. You must be receptive and nondefensive, or you risk helping the issue to become much bigger than it now is.

"In former times, people would often enter a monastery if they wanted to explore the deeper mysteries of life. For many of us today, however, intimate relationship has become the new wilderness that brings us face to face with all our Gods and all our demons."
(John Wellwood)

BUILDING A CASE AGAINST YOUR PARTNER

Dear Neil: I spend a fair amount of time angry at my husband. When I'm alone, I silently say to myself that my husband has hurt me or disappointed me or angered me—and I think of all the things he has done in our seventeen years together that fit those emotions. I then started sharing these emotions about my husband with several close girlfriends of mine. That way no one gets hurt, and I get to vent, commiserate with others and receive support for my feelings. Recently I shared with my husband some of the things us girls have been talking about, and he got furious. He said that I was violating his trust and hurting our marriage. I said no I'm not; I'm just venting to friends. This has caused a rift between us. Do you have an opinion?

—No Harm Meant in Connecticut

Dear Connecticut: It can be helpful to work out how you feel about an issue by talking with others. Nothing is wrong with talking things out with other people—that's indeed what most counselors and therapists do for a living. But you have to be careful, because your husband could easily feel that you are revealing things to friends that may feel personal and private to him, and you don't want him to feel that you have breached trust or have publicly undressed him.

There are actually three issues here. First, that you are sharing information with other people that he would consider personal, private, and confidential. Second, you are in the habit of consistently building a case against your husband in your own head. That means that from time to time, you look for more evidence to support your feelings or to justify how you feel. A short step later you will begin to prepare a speech in your head in which you accuse, try, and convict your husband of wrongdoing, or of being insensitive, selfish, or inadequate.

You are now painting a portrait of your husband as the bad guy in your marriage. But by doing so, you diminish the good feelings you have for him and therefore cause yourself to feel even worse. When you feel bad about him, you will also feel bad about yourself, because you are committed to him. You are "making a case" against your husband, as if you were in a court of law and he was on trial. But if you win this trial you also lose, because you have now worked yourself into an unhappy state with someone you presumably also love, care about, and want to feel closer to. I don't think doing this is in your own best interests.

Third, the one thing left out of your letter is any attempt to repair the relationship with your husband, and to work through all the hurt, anger, and disappointed feelings you have about him. You're not telling him how you feel; you're telling girlfriends. And no matter how much your girlfriends commiserate with you, they can't fix these problems.

But your husband could, and that becomes the solution to your dilemma. Tell him what's bugging you. But instead of just complaining, tell him also what you'd like him to do differently.

It's the only way you're going to heal your marriage.

"One of the best things about marriage is that it gets young people to bed at a decent hour." (M. M. Musselman)

COUPLE'S EXERCISE IN FEELING CLOSER AND MORE CONNECTED

Can you hear feelings and opinions about yourself without becoming defensive? Can you hear honest feedback from someone you love or care about, or do you force loved ones to walk on eggshells around you so as not to offend you? This article is going to challenge you to talk—and listen—openly and honestly with your spouse, lover, or intimate partner and not get defensive, reactive, or angry.

When we share our innermost feelings and talk intimately, most of us feel closer and more connected with each other. So why do I bring up defensiveness in this discussion? Because that's the easiest and quickest way to sabotage the questions that follow. If you become defensive or upset at hearing your partner's open and honest answers to personal and intimate questions—frequently thought but not spoken—exactly how close do you think your relationship is going to get?

So honor this good-faith rule before you address the following questions as a couple: no defensiveness, anger, vindictive responses, or hostility allowed. This exercise is designed to help the two of you feel closer, not more distant. If you cannot hear what your intimate partner truly feels and thinks, your relationship will never feel solid and strong. These questions come from *365 Questions for Couples* by Michael, Stanis and Seanna Beck (Adams Media Corporation):

- Do you believe I know myself well?
- What is your favorite thing about my personality?
- What, if anything, have you learned from me?
- If you could plan a trip for us to anyplace in the world, where would you choose to take us?
- What is your favorite memory about our relationship?
- In what ways do you feel I could make your life easier or more comfortable? What changes or adjustments would I have to make?
- What, if anything, do you feel you need to sacrifice or compromise by being a part of our relationship?
- How well do you think I handle myself when I'm in a crisis situation?
- Do you think that I manage problems in our relationship well?
- What do you suggest I do in order to enjoy life more? Are there any changes you believe I should make?
- What do you suggest I do in order to better enjoy my career? Are there any changes you believe I could make?
- What, if anything, do you suggest I do in order to relax and enjoy our relationship more?

- Is there any topic you wish I was more open about?
- In what areas do you think we need to improve our relationship? Do you believe these changes are possible, or do you think we will always struggle with these issues?
- What are your basic expectations of a partner? Of me as a partner?
- Are there any minor changes that I could make to my appearance to make myself more attractive?
- Do you think I have a lot in common with other members of my family? Who do I most closely take after, and in which ways?
- What would you say if you could only communicate one last sentence to me for the rest of eternity? What would you like me to say to you?
- How do you feel our relationship helps and/or hinders the fulfillment of your goals?
- List the five things you appreciate about me the most. The five things about me that annoy you the most.
- Is there anything about me that reminds you of your mother or father? How about past lovers or close friends?
- What similarities in our backgrounds do you think contribute to the strength of our relationship? What differences (in values, religion, culture, siblings, interests, or experiences) would you consider to be hard on us?
- What are my talents? What are yours?

- In what ways do you think I can help you with the problems or struggles in your life?
- In what ways do you believe you can help me to become a better person?
- How important do you think you are to me? Do you think my life would be equally happy and successful without you?
- What do you like about my physical features? Which one do you like the best?
- Is there anything I do that makes you uncomfortable?
- Am I usually able to read and interpret the signals that you send? Which ones do I get correctly, and where do I need to improve?
- In which ways do you think we are alike? How are we different from one another?

"Why should human females become sterile in their forties, while female crocodiles continue to lay eggs into their third century?" (Aldous Huxley)

CHOOSING PEACE INSTEAD OF IRRITATION

Dear Neil: How would you recommend I handle this? My wife of three months is chronically late. She was late to our wedding and late to our honeymoon (we missed our flight, but we were able to get a later flight). I'm one of these super-punctual people, and her persistent lateness is a strong irritation for me in our marriage.

But the irritation doesn't stop there. She also goes to bed at 8 pm, which is way too early for me. This means I go to bed when she's asleep, and she wakes up when I'm asleep, and we operate on largely different schedules. She's also far messier than I am, and it bothers me when our place looks unkempt and sloppy.

I love her and I'm devoted to her, and I recognize that none of these are deal breakers. But they are irritants that get in my way from feeling consistently loving and close toward her. How would you recommend I handle this?

—Irritated in California

Dear California: Welcome to the not-always-rewarding experience of trying to blend lives, values, schedules, and habits with someone else. If you had chosen to marry the lady next door, the woman down the street or a lady in another country, you would likely have equal or greater irritants with those women as you do with the one you married. The nature of two people living together ensures that the two of you will get on each other's nerves from time to time.

Marriage is about two people trying to live together harmoniously and civilly with each other. It's not like the two of you value all the same things or are clones of each other. It's about two people trying to function as one, not one person's way to the exclusion of the other.

There is a happy way out of this dilemma. It's about choosing to be peaceful rather than being irritated at your wife.

Yes, of course it can be alarming to miss your flight on your honeymoon, especially if you have a connecting flight to meet. So, knowing that your new wife is time-challenged, why don't you take charge in the future of when you need to be at the airport (and any other important functions) so the two of you can be on time when it really counts. Tell your wife you would like to be in charge of helping the two of you be on time for important events, and ask for her cooperation and agreement. If she agrees, then take on that task without getting angry, annoyed, critical, or judgmental toward her.

But in addition to solving this problem, choose to be at peace with her rather than in a cold war with her. At any given moment, we have the ability to choose peace over irritation, even though it doesn't always seem like it. That's because our reactions seem to be instantaneous, and it doesn't seem as if we have a lot of control over them.

But we actually do have control over them. We're just not always that adept and skillful at exercising good control over our reactions and judgments. You indeed have a choice about how you wish to respond to what your wife (or anyone else) says or does. To choose peace rather than irritation allows you to be happier, more serene, and calmer, and it also creates an environment with considerately less conflict, discord, tension, and *brain damage,* everything else being equal.

I'm not saying that you shouldn't attempt to help your wife leave 30 minutes earlier to an appointment, or that the two of you shouldn't make agreements to keep the house clean and tidy. I'm saying that you have the power and the ability to respond differently whenever your wife irritates you or lets you down. It's empowering to make a loving and peaceful choice instead of an angry, reactive, or judgmental choice—and she is bound to feel less judged and criticized by you—and therefore closer and more intimate with you.

Try this out: the next time your wife says or does something that would normally irritate you, consciously go to a peaceful, loving, and harmonious response. If she's late, find a constructive or productive way to occupy yourself until she shows up, and don't allow yourself to get angry or irritated. If she leaves the kitchen a mess, ask how you can help her clean it up.

Choose peace rather than irritation whenever you can. You'll be a happier guy, and you'll be easier to live with.

"I want to tell you a terrific story about oral contraception.
I asked this girl to sleep with me and she said "no." (Woody Allen)

THE "SECRETS" OF COMPATIBILITY

Dear Neil: My fiancé and I are fighting a lot with each other, and that's thrown our wedding—scheduled for later this year—into serious question. Is there a secret for how to know if we can be compatible with each other? We have a lot of common interests and similar tastes in music, Italian food, and gourmet coffees. How can we have compatibility, also?

—Not Getting Along in Westminster, Colorado

Dear Not Getting Along: Compatibility isn't something you have. It's something the two of you make. The similarities and personality traits that attract two people to each other—such as common tastes in music, art, travel, and food—is what gets you together, not what typically keeps you together.

Here are some of the most important behaviors and attitudes that two people must cultivate and develop over time in order for them to feel compatible with each other:

- **Treating the other person with respect.** This includes the assumption of good will, the absence of malice, and the benefit of doubt.

- **Open and skilled communication.** Compatible couples share their secrets, personal intimacies, delights, thoughts, feelings, hopes, wishes, hurts, frustrations, disappointments, yearnings, and fears with each other. Good communication is reciprocal sharing, which is more than just bombarding someone with your thoughts and feelings. It is also about knowing the difference between "talking at" and "talking with" someone; being interested and inquisitive about the other person's emotions, needs, and desires; being an extremely good listener; and hearing the other person's feelings without being defensive, hostile, or dismissive.

- **Compatible couples have figured out healthy, positive ways of dealing with grievances, disagreements, disappointments, and past wounds.** This includes good conflict resolution, problem solving, negotiating, and compromising skills—and these skills must be used continually throughout the relationship.

- **Trust.** This includes being faithful and loyal, and helping your mate in feeling secure about your loyalty. Any breeches of trust are worked through and resolved right away.

- **Compatible couples spend time together.** They tend to do things with each other. They make their intimate relationship a top priority in their lives.

- **Being responsive.** Make what's important to him/her important to you.

- **There is a sense of true partnership between equals.** Major decisions are made jointly. Both believe that the division of labor is fair as it relates to roles, chores, and housework.

- **Romance.** Reach out to your partner and be receptive and responsive when s/he reaches out to you. Go out of your way to please—and do so on an ongoing basis. Include lots of non-sexual touch, hand holding, hugs, and cuddling.
- **Sex.** Be a willing sexual partner, and try to please each other.
- **Honesty.** Say what you mean and mean what you say. Keep your word, your promises, and your agreements.
- **Friendship and support.** You feel your partner generally is your friend and ally—and you can turn to him/her for emotional support.
- **Having fun** together on a regular basis.
- Compatible couples do everything they can to **stay emotionally connected with each other.**
- Compatible people both **have easy, congenial temperaments,** and they value getting along.

"Relationships are hard. It's like a full time job, and we should treat it like one. If your boyfriend or girlfriend wants to leave you, they should give you two weeks' notice. There should be severance pay, and before they leave you, they should find you a temp."
(Bob Ettinger)

HAVING MORE FUN IS ONE WAY TO KEEP THE ROMANCE ALIVE

Most of the time, the couple that plays together, stays together.

Once a relationship has a commitment, people tend to quit dating—and the fun slows way down. What we then have is a variety of responsibilities and obligations—all of the things we "have to" do in order to sustain a relationship, family, home, and career and get the bills paid.

But most people who quit dating also quit regularly having fun together. One of the problems of doing fun things together is that two people frequently have differing ideas about what constitute fun. Some people find board games (Monopoly, Rumicube, Scrabble) entertaining, while others may find such games boring. Some people would be enormously challenged and excited by learning a foreign language, while others would find it too much work. Some people find watching a sports event enjoyable, while others do not. Many people watch TV as their main form of fun. But most of the time, TV is not fun: It is a way of zoning out, and most people are not having fun while they are watching TV.

For me, the concept of fun has changed over the years. I used to find concerts, ballets, and plays enjoyable. At some point it became much less fun to do those things. When I look at what I now find fun, it usually involves my active—rather than passive participation—things like hiking, tennis, canoeing, dancing, and traveling (although I still like watching action movies).

Recent research on the subject confirms that couples who would like to have more fun would be well advised to learn how to date again. You may need to relearn that there are many interesting, exciting, and stimulating things to do that can recharge you as a couple, and prevent you from growing stale together. You could look at the various ways the two of you can continuously infuse novelty into your relationship.

Here's how to put these ideas to work:

First, each of you create a list titled "What Fun?" Be as expansive as you can. Include at least a dozen items—three dozen if possible. Second, create a second list titled "New Things I Would Like to Experience, Experiment with, or Try." Again, include as many items as you can. Share your respective lists, and create a third list of all the activities or new experiences you agree on together.

Now combine your two lists with your partner's, and come up with a joint list of five fun things you will commit to doing together during the next month or two, and another five things you will commit to doing with each other over the next four to five months. Then create one more joint list of several additional fun things you will commit to doing together during the next twelve months. All of these must be jointly agreed upon. Keep the two joint lists very visible—say, posted on a mirror or the refrigerator—because the reminders will help the two of you to remember what you've agreed to.

Continuously update these lists. Don't let yourself get into a rut. Keep on experimenting with new things (miniature golf, card games, weekend getaway trips, joining a choir, skiing, water-skiing, gardening, Frisbee, bowling, walking or running in a 5k or 10K race, taking a tango class together, tennis—you get the idea. Planning such events and activities gives you new experiences to look forward to on an ongoing basis, and it helps things to be more interesting—and interest often translates into romance.

"I love being married. I was single for a long time, and I just got so sick of finishing my own sentences." Brian Kelly

PERSONAL POWER DOESN'T REQUIRE ANGER

Dear Neil: What's been fascinating for me is to realize how ill-equipped I am to having any reaction other than anger—or feeling like a doormat. Learning to rein in anger is freeing, but if people who have relied on anger for power don't have any other readily available choices besides capitulating, it can lead to a crippling sense of impotence and powerlessness. Without my anger, I became a neutered person around my wife, because I simply do not have the skills to find an alternative between my anger and submission. I'd love to see you write about how I can find my power without resorting to anger.

—Curious In Boulder

Dear Curious: Your first and most important solution is to know what your feelings and needs are—and to effectively communicate them to your wife before you get angry or reactive. If you do that, you don't have to resort to anger in order to speak up about what you feel, need, or want.

So when you first notice you're beginning to get angry, and before you allow yourself to get really worked up and hostile, take a brief (thirty minute) time out and ask yourself the following questions: What else am I feeling other than anger right now? How vulnerable do I feel? About what? Am I feeling shamed? About what? Am I feeling criticized, judged, or inadequate? About what? Might this anger be deliberate—as a device for getting my way—or for distancing when things get too close, intimate, or threatening? Am I attempting to cover up my feelings of inadequacy or low self-esteem with my anger?

Second, challenge yourself to communicate your emotions in a more skilled, effective fashion, by addressing these questions with your wife: When I get upset, I'd like for you to respond to me by ... I feel invalidated, hurt or not cared for when ... When you're being critical, I would be less sensitive if you would also ... I could be more vulnerable around you if you would ...I could assist myself in feeling understood if I were to ... I could better understand you if I were to ... Please forgive me for ... To resolve this issue, I need ....

Then invite your wife to respond to the same questions, with you, giving her a full respectful hearing—so both of you can address what you feel, need, and want.

The purpose of this exercise is to learn how to confront problems, issues, or conflicts as they arise with skill and finesse, without having to resort to angry explosions, hurtful comments, or bad vibes.

I'm not saying there isn't an appropriate place for anger. There is. But personal power doesn't come from angry explosions, even if you sometimes get your way by using anger. Personal power comes from having a skilled, effective way of expressing yourself—and then doing it.

"Instead of getting married again, I'm going to find a woman I don't like and just give her a house." (Lewis Grizzard)

LEARN TO HOLD YOURSELF ACCOUNTABLE FOR YOUR ANGRY OUTBURSTS

Dear Neil: I know I have an anger problem and I need help to control it. When things don't work out, when I'm running late or when I've taken too much on, I can turn into a monster. I snap and yell at my kids, and I say the most terrible things to them that I bitterly regret afterwards. I always apologize later, explaining why I was angry and telling them it wasn't their fault, but I feel I'm damaging them emotionally.

I have a lot of anger inside of me because I was emotionally abused as a child. I was made to feel that I was a loser, an idiot, and unattractive. I need some strategies to help me recognize when that anger is threatening to bubble over. Also, it's difficult to walk away when I'm in the car or when I am awakened by my son three times in the middle of the night. What can I do?

—Angry in Manchester, United Kingdom

Dear Angry: The first thing you can do to control your anger is to quit making excuses and offering self-justifications for blowing your top. We can all come up with loads of excuses for why we can lose our temper ("you're irritating me," "I've already answered that question," "I've had a hard day at work, so don't get on my bad side tonight," and so on).Your childhood may indeed be why you have a lot of anger inside, but your childhood is not making you lose your temper. You're adopting the attitude that your children are responsible for your explosions, that they are, in essence, forcing you to be angry because they won't abide by your wishes or your rules, or because they are acting irritating.

But your children are not responsible for your emotional reactions. You are. That's where you can begin exerting control over your temper: by accepting responsibility for everything you say or do when you're angry, irritated or upset, and by holding yourself accountable for more tolerant, loving behavior.

Second, when you feel your temperature starting to rise, step back and ask yourself the following questions: What is the emotion underneath my anger? (Hurt? Fear? Feeling invisible? Feeling devalued? Feeling inadequate? Feeling overwhelmed?) Specifically, what is it that is triggering me? Other than anger, what am I feeling right now? (Vulnerable? Shamed? Inadequate? Impotent? Powerless?) What do I want to see happen? What do I need in order to resolve this issue?

If you ask yourself these questions before you react, you will be starting to gain greater control over your anger, because the answers to the above questions are likely driving your temper outbursts.

Third, let's assume you're right, that your upbringing has a lot to do with why you're so angry. If you grow up feeling badly about yourself, you will likely, as an adult, be relentlessly self-critical, highly self-blaming, have low levels of self-love and poor self-acceptance. In essence, you will endlessly brood about how disappointing you are, how unworthy you feel, how unlovable you believe yourself to be, and how flawed you are. If this is what you're doing, no wonder you feel so angry. Now it's not just the memories of childhood that are driving you. This time around, it's you who are telling yourself how much of a loser you are. If this is accurate, you need a psychotherapist to help you work on overcoming childhood messages and improving your self-esteem and sense of self-worth.

Fourth, learn to stop escalating and to calm yourself instead. Close your eyes and focus on your breathing. Take regular, long, slow, deep breaths until you feel calmer and less on edge. There are a variety of meditative techniques you could learn, all of which focus on relaxing your overactive mind or calming your edginess. I am saying that you have the power and the ability to respond differently when your children irritate you, and it would be empowering for both you and your kids if you responded in a peaceful manner rather than in an angry, reactive, or judgmental manner.

There is no excuse for you not being a more loving, patient and tolerant mother. There is no excuse for you to turn ugly or to hurt the people you care about. Hold yourself accountable for learning how to be in control of you. If you do, you will reduce the likelihood of you doing to your children what was done to you.

"I tended to place my wife under a pedestal." (Woody Allen)

BREAKING A POWER STRUGGLE

Eric and Candy, who have been together two years, are not getting along. Candy says she needs more emotional support and sensitivity. Eric wants a more willing and nurturing lover. Neither of them feels that their needs are being met by the other, and both of them are refusing to give what the other person has asked for until their needs are attended to first.

Sound familiar? In fact, an intimate relationship is our emotional attempt to get our lifelong needs and desires met that were not met earlier in life.

To have a relationship with another person means you are also having a relationship with the person's past—and his/her lifelong pain, hurts, angers, fears, and disappointments. Most people are looking for someone to repair the past. They are seeking the nurturing and approval that will, in essence, compensate for what they did not get growing up.

You are just trying to work through unresolved issues and unmet needs from childhood—in an attempt to satisfy your lifelong desire for approval, affection, attention, and love. But your partner, typically, has no idea that he or she is expected to compensate for what you went through long ago.

In the beginning of a relationship, we are more open to giving and being receptive to the other person's needs and desires. After the relationship progresses and stabilizes, each person's needs and unmet lifelong desires emerge.

At that point, we cease primarily wanting to be caregivers in the relationship, and we expect and feel entitled to finally become care receivers. Now it is our turn to get our needs met. The only problem with that is that our partners are thinking, feeling, and expecting the same thing. Now two people expect that it's their turn to receive, and both feel entitled.

You can guess what happens then: both people will feel cheated. Both feel the other is intentionally withholding what they rightfully deserve and have waited patiently for all these years to receive.

In most intimate relationships, there's an unacknowledged and unspoken exchange: I'll give you what you want if you'll give me what I want. If, therefore, I feel you're not meeting my needs, I may respond by refusing to give you what I know you want. The relationship then becomes a power struggle between the two parties over whose needs and desires take priority. Unfortunately, there are no winners in this battle. Both people feel righteous and justified in blaming the other person for the lack of closeness in their relationship.

There's a way out of this trap. It's about doing what we are so resistant to: giving the other person what s/he most wants. You could single handedly break the impasse between the two of you and give your partner what s/he wants—without asking for anything in return. In other words, you could unlink what you're giving from what you want to receive, thus ending the tired, old, dead-end power struggles between the two of you.

What is the essence of what s/he needs or has been asking for? This could be the opportunity for the two of you to break into a brand-new level of intimacy, closeness and happiness.

"I want a man who's kind and understanding. Is that too much to ask of a millionaire?" (Zsa Zsa Gabor)

WARM FUZZIES AND COLD PRICKLIES

I remember hearing this tale years ago. I am recounting it here to the best of my memory.

Once upon a time, in a faraway land, there was a village in which everyone acted considerate, polite, and friendly toward each other.

Walking down the street of this village, you would be likely to hear one person say "That's a lovely suit you have on." and the response, "Thank you. You played so well in the orchestra last night. You're really good." Another conversation might sound like this: "I'm delighted to see you today." and the response, "I'm looking forward to working with you again."

The people of the village talked this way with everybody. If you looked carefully at them when they talked, you would notice that after each person said something nice to the other, a warm fuzzy was exchanged between the two of them.

A warm fuzzy is called that because it feels, well, warm and fuzzy when you receive one. Warm fuzzies take up almost no room, so you can have many with you at the same time. There is an unlimited number of warm fuzzies, so regardless of how many you give away, you never run out.

One day a grinch moved into town. The grinch was uncomfortable when someone from the village greeted him warmly or complimented him. He had not come from an environment where people did that with each other, and he felt jealous and envious of the other people. So the grinch devised a strategy in order to stop people from giving warm fuzzies to each other.

The next morning, as the grinch walked down the street of the village, a stranger walked up to him and said, "Good morning, Mr. Grinch. My, you seem like an interesting person. I am looking forward to getting to know you better," and handed the grinch a warm fuzzy.

The grinch put his plan into action. He said to the stranger, "Why are you offering me one of your valuable warm fuzzies? Don't you know there is a shortage of warm fuzzies these days? You're going to give all of them away, and then you'll have none left for yourself. Here, there are lots of these. Take some, and pass these around instead." The grinch handed the man some cold pricklies. Cold pricklies have that name because they feel, well, cold and prickly to receive.

The man, who had not heard of a shortage of warm fuzzies, took the cold pricklies and left. A few minutes later, when someone from the village complimented the man on his warm smile, he kept the warm fuzzy offered him and handed the person a cold prickly in return by saying: "You're always saying syrupy, sweet things. You should learn to be more balanced with what you say to others."

As news of the shortage of warm fuzzies spread around town, people throughout the village ran home and hid their warm fuzzies for safekeeping, and collected large numbers of cold pricklies to use instead.

Walking down the street of this village quit being a warm and fuzzy experience—and instead became a cold prickly experience. One person would say to another, "Your dress doesn't look good on you." to which the response might be, 'You're growing more wrinkles around the eyes." Each would then give the other a cold prickly.

The Grinch observed that the entire village was growing unfriendly. He felt satisfied with what he had done. He had been very uncomfortable when everyone was warm and friendly to each other. People who are unfamiliar with giving and receiving warm fuzzies want compliments and encouragement more than anything, but they're awkward with friendliness and need some practice with it.

The whole community became unfriendly, critical, and sour. People quit talking to each other and kept to themselves. You'd just get cold pricklies from conversations with others. People grew tired of feeling disliked and of being criticized.

One day, a young man decided he couldn't bear the loneliness anymore and called the entire community together to talk about what could be done.

When the meeting began, the young man got up and did something nobody expected: He passed out warm fuzzies to everyone there. He said things such as, "Hello, Mrs. Smith. You have such a friendly face." and "Hi Sam, I really respect how hard you've been working lately," and "I'm really looking forward to hearing you play the piano again, Susie." Each person he spoke to got a warm fuzzy.

People were stunned. There was a shortage of warm fuzzies, and here was a young man freely giving all of his warm fuzzies away. Someone said: "Be careful or you won't have any left for yourself."

The young man responded, "Why is it that we used to pass out warm fuzzies all the time and never ran out before? Who says there's a shortage? What good are warm fuzzies if you hoard them all and are afraid to use them?"

A little girl stood up and said, in a very quiet voice: "Thank you for doing this." She then hugged the young man, took a crumpled warm fuzzy from her pocket, and gave it to him.

The villagers talked well into the night. They figured out that it was the Grinch who had started the rumor that there was a warm fuzzy shortage, and they devised a strategy to deal with him.

The next morning, when the Grinch walked down the street, someone said to him, "Hello, Mr. Grinch. You look lovely today," and handed the Grinch a warm fuzzy. Before the Grinch could react, another person said: "My wife and I would like to invite you over to dinner so we can get to know you better," and handed the Grinch another warm fuzzy. In fact, everyone in the village came up to the Grinch, said something warm and friendly, and gave him a warm fuzzy.

The Grinch was so caught off guard that he started to cry. Big tears rolled down his cheeks, and all he could say was, "I've never known people who actually tried to like me before."

If you had strolled down the streets of the village after that day, you would have been greeted by people who would go out of their way to say nice things to you, and you would have received many, many warm fuzzies.

The Grinch decided to destroy all the cold pricklies that he had created. He was learning how to have friends and how to be a friend, and he was a much happier person.

"There will be sex after death; we just won't be able to feel it."
(Lily Tomlin)

THE LOSS OF SEXUAL DESIRE

Dear Neil: I am a thirty-eight-year-old married mother of two, and I have an issue with the total loss of my sexual desire. We have a good marriage. I love my husband dearly and I am very attracted to him. I don't know what it wrong with me. I have no desire to have sex at all. Can you help me? I don't want to lose him, and he has been very patient with me.

—It's Not Working Right in Colorado

Dear Not Working Right: There could be any number of things going on within you that could influence your libido. Therefore, perhaps the only way I can be of help to you is to pose questions for you to explore, and see if you yourself can isolate the factors effecting your loss of sexual desire. All of these factors can contribute to loss of sexual desire:

- Are you depressed?
- Are you grieving the loss of anybody or anything, even the loss of a self-image?

- Are you taking any sedatives, diuretics, prescription medications, recreational drugs or are you drinking large volumes of alcohol?
- Other than sexually, how's your self-esteem, sense of self-worth, and sense of self-confidence?
- Do you have any health issues you're currently dealing with? Are you in physical pain or do you feel ill?
- How is your weight and level of exercise/activity? When you look in the mirror, do you see yourself as attractive, appealing, and sexy?
- Do you have trust issues from your past?
- What do you need—and how much time do you need—in order to warm up sexually? Are you and your husband allowing time for adequate foreplay?
- Are you getting enough sleep? Might you be chronically fatigued or tired a lot?
- Are you angry, and if so, what are you angry about? Might you be angry with your husband?
- Could you and your husband be in a power struggle? Do you feel controlled by him? Could you be punishing your husband for something? Are the two of you competing against each other?
- Do you have a fear of being taken over, of losing yourself, of being used or dominated?

- Are you feeling blamed, judged, or criticized a lot, or are you otherwise being made to feel as if you're inadequate?
- Is there a lot of hostility in your relationship?
- Do you reach orgasm when you do have sex ? Is the sexual experience enjoyable for you?
- Are you under a lot of stress?
- Other than sexually, how close are you and your husband? How romantic is your relationship? How affectionate? How much friendship, consideration, and camaraderie is there? How well do the two of you kiss? Do you open up and share your inner worlds and feelings with each other?
- What's going wrong with your life in general, and how well are you dealing with it?
- Do the two of you treat each other with kindness and respect?

If none of these questions assist you, perhaps you should get a complete physical with a blood workup, and ask your physician if he/she can determine anything medically that may be influencing your libido.

Be willing to acknowledge to your husband that you're aware that there's a problem, and that you're doing everything you can to solve it. And reassure him that you're not trying to reject him.

"Sex between a man and a woman can be wonderful, provided you can get between the right man and the right woman." (Woody Allen)

HOW TO JUMP START YOUR LOVE LIFE

Dear Neil: I am in a long-term mostly happy marriage with my husband of seventeen years, but there is no sexual juice at all between us. In virtually every other respect our relationship is wonderful: we love and care about each other, we are financially doing OK, we're good parents together, we're very compatible, we get along well, we seldom fight or even disagree. He is attractive and successful, our doctors say that we're both healthy and fit, and we are very social with other people. So what is wrong with us? We seldom are romantic, we haven't been sexual in a long time, and we're the opposite of "hot and juicy." But we used to be extremely charged with each other. Is this what middle age does to everyone, or are we doing something wrong?

—Going Without in Los Angeles

Dear Los Angeles: What you're describing sounds like a lack of romantic and sexual effort. It's not about being middle aged—biologically you guys may have slowed down a bit, but you're not dead yet, and couples can enjoy each other sexually well into their nineties if they remain healthy and vital.

But the day-in and day-out routine that gets established in a long-term relationship can be very deadening to eroticism. Work, commuting, and daily chores or responsibilities can preoccupy us, kids can be needy and demanding, and keeping a home, paying bills, preparing meals, doing laundry, and hundreds of other tasks can use us up very quickly and make us very tired—if not exhausted.

Couples that remain hot and juicy often have to work at it—it's not like when you were in your twenties and it was the only show in town. I'm saying that oftentimes adult sex requires conscious effort, romantic words, and gestures, complimenting your partner on his "sexiness," affectionate touch, cuddling, seductive invitations, weekend romantic getaways, and other such behaviors.

While you're at it, go out and buy a hot little lingerie number, and surprise him with it. (You don't need to worry about it being uncomfortable—it won't stay on very long.) Then call him on the phone at work. Verify that it is a private call and nobody else can hear your conversation. And then proceed to tell him, in intimate detail, exactly what you will do with him when he gets home and you guys have some alone free time—or tell him what you would like him to do to you.

This is what I mean when I refer to putting romantic and sexual effort into your relationship. Staying romantically engaged doesn't happen on its own; it requires your intention, foresight, effort and persistence. Here are some additional suggestions on how to keep things hot and juicy:

Make time for your love life. Don't let other priorities push it to last place, and don't wait until you're really tired.

Find a book illustrating different positions. See if you can try every one of them. That will keep things from growing stale, familiar or old.

Create sexual "dates" with your husband, and say "yes" when you're approached most of the time. Men who are rejected often quit trying, and then they are far more likely to seethe in anger and resentment.

Leave suggestive or seductive notes, voice mail messages, texts, or emails telling him you think he's hot, sexy and attractive—and that you want him.

Teach your husband what he needs to do in order to help you get in the mood. Tell him specifically what you want or need—emotionally, verbally, how much affection, what feels romantic to you, how you want to be touched and held and kissed—and don't assume he knows.

If you are hurt or angry with him, tell him why, and tell him what you need in order for that hurt or anger to lessen.

Take the lead. Men love it when women initiate and act seductive. Tell him you want him and put his hands on your body.

"My wife kisses the dog on the lips, yet she won't drink from my glass." (Rodney Dangerfield)

WHAT OUR INTIMATE RELATIONSHIPS TEACH US

If you're wise, you'll view your intimate relationships—and your partner—as a teacher of yours.

Relationships have essential lessons to teach, and you must learn them if you are to have a fulfilling intimate life:

- Happiness in a relationship is not just a question of finding the right partner. It's also a matter of being the right partner by being willing to blend; being in charge of your anger, reactivity, and defensiveness; and being respectful, giving affection, love, forgiveness, commitment, fidelity, acting trustworthy and reliable.

- In intimate communication, there is feeling and a fact. We say: "I feel this about that." If you're going to miss anything in that communication, miss the fact. Do not miss the feeling, because the feeling is what matters.

- You can find an excellent reason to reject everyone—alive or dead—on this planet. The trick is to find—and to continue to find—reasons for staying together.

- You can't withdraw when you're hurt or angry. Withdrawal is the death knell of an intimate relationship. Withdrawal kills intimacy. Far better for you to say you are upset, angry, or hurt and to attempt to talk it through. You must learn to not put up a wall if you want a close intimate relationship.

- Touch is the greatest aphrodisiac that exists. It helps us to get close, feel close, and stay close. If you're not touching each other a lot, your relationship is unlikely to feel hot and passionate, and both of you will notice that the closeness and connection you once had has waned. I'm talking about affectionate touch, not sexual touch—although one often leads to the other.

- Ask yourself: "If I were going to make this relationship work, what would I need to do? What would I need to quit doing?" Most people know what they want from their intimate partner, but few people have a clear perspective about what their partner needs or wants from them. If you don't know the answer to this question—or if your answers are superficial or vague—ask your partner: "Are you getting your needs met in this relationship? (And if not, what would you like different?)" Then do your best to honor what your intimate partner says matters.

- When your mate is angry, s/he is usually feeling hurt underneath that anger. Ask why s/he is feeling hurt. That's how you can diffuse anger.

- Stop complaining to friends and family about your relationship. If you have a problem, go directly to your mate.

- If you want your relationship to work, you have to make it your conscious intention and purpose to make it work. In order for romance to stay alive, you have to keep it alive.

- If your mate doesn't feel cherished by you, your relationship will feel less intimate and less connected. What behaviors would make your partner feel cherished? Ask this question. Do it now.

If you think about it, some of your greatest lessons have come from your intimate relationships. It's how we grow; how we gain wisdom and maturity. Your relationships have something to teach you about how things work and how you are expected to behave. With every misstep or error that you make, ask yourself: "What is the lesson in this for me? What can this teach me?"

You are likely to discover that many of life's lessons are centered around your intimate relationships with those people close to you, especially your spouse/intimate partner and your children.

"To love is to suffer. To avoid suffering one must not love. But then one suffers from not loving. Therefore, to love is to suffer; not to love is to suffer; and to suffer is to suffer. To be happy is to love. To be happy, then, is to suffer, but suffering makes one unhappy. Therefore, to be happy one must love or love to suffer or suffer from too much happiness." (Woody Allen)

HUSBANDRY 101

Dear Neil: I have saved a column you wrote over a decade ago called "Husbandry 101: For Committed Men." My copy has yellowed and frayed over the years, so could you rerun that column again? I believe many would like to see it again.

—Boulder, Colorado

Dear Boulder: You bet. Here is a list of "rules" that every committed man would be wise to follow in his intimate relationship:

- Never forget what's really important. Despite all the challenges that we face with our careers, paying the bills, and surviving, it is our relationship issues that cause us the most challenge, pain, excitement, satisfaction, joy, and heartbreak. Our relationships, in the end, are the only things that really matter—the relationships we have with our spouses, parents, children, siblings, in-laws, friends—and the relationship we have with ourselves.
- You must give to your marriage more than you expect to receive from it. Learn this—and form the habits of giving, pleasing, serving, nurturing, being affectionate, romancing. If you

take more than you give, the reservoir of trust, good will, generosity, and love will dry up.

- Women want to feel cherished. That's more important than virtually anything else you can offer.
- Ask for what you want in concrete, specific terms and give up whining, manipulating, punishing, withholding, or withdrawing in order to get your way.
- Take responsibility for making your relationship right. It's up to each of us to take the actions required to make our relationship happy, vital, passionate, and close. So search for the solutions to the dilemmas and conflicts in your relationship. When you look for solutions, you'll usually be able to find them. Accept the leadership role in keeping the relationship close and clearing up anything in the way of the two of you being close.
- Learn the art of how to apologize genuinely. Admit when you are wrong, do whatever is necessary to make it right, and then don't do it again.
- Ask these questions: How am I doing as your partner/mate/husband? What are the ways I could improve? Are your needs getting met in our relationship? If not, what would you like me to do differently?
- If you want a happy, long-term intimate relationship, learn good problem-solving, negotiating, conflict resolution, anger management, and compromising skills—and apply them.
- A happy woman will influence your happiness more than you'll ever know. An unhappy woman will create an unhappy

environment, and it will eventually sour you and everyone else around you. If you wish to have a happy home, do everything you can to keep your woman happy.

- The key to creating the best relationship you possibly can is to learn how to take your wall down and open your heart.
- Always be a lover in training. Always be a "student" husband—constantly willing to learn or take feedback about how you could be better.
- Learn how to be a true friend to your partner. Ask yourself: if I were saying this to my best friend, how would I show I care? What would I say? How well would I listen? How would I help?
- Loving her isn't enough. You must also be skilled, tactful, balanced, kind, generous, compassionate, and emotionally and physically present.
- Adopt this motto: The only purpose of this relationship is for me to learn how to become a more loving person.
- Thank the woman in your life for all she has contributed to you. Do this right now.

"Brevity may be the soul of wit, but not when someone is saying 'I love you.' When someone is saying 'I love you,' he ought to give a lot of details, like why does he love you, and how much does he love you and when and where did he first begin to love you. Favorable comparisons with all the other women he ever loved also are welcomed, and even though he insists it would take forever to count the ways in which he loves you, you would not want to discourage him from counting." (Judith Viorst)

RULES FOR WOMEN IN A COMMITTED RELATIONSHIP

Dear Neil: I was wondering if you have a Wife 101 column to go with your Husbandry 101 column. What are the equivalent rules for women?

—Committed Lady in Australia

Dear Australia: Here they are.

Many women adopt a passive attitude toward romance; they tend to think of courtship, romance and seduction as something a man does to them. It's a man's job to woo you and make you feel valued, cherished, and beautiful. It's a man's job to bring you flowers, open doors for you, compliment you, wine and dine you, and seduce you.

But in truth, romance works best when it is reciprocal. Reciprocal romance means that a woman also needs to woo her man, as well as court him, nurture him, support him, and encourage him. She also needs to be a seductress, not just the seduced.

The following is a list of rules for women who are committed to being the best wife or girlfriend they can be. If you do your very best in your relationship day in and day out, you'll be a happier woman, you'll reduce the chance that he might cheat, you'll increase the probability of the two of you staying together, you'll be a great role model for your children, and you will have achieved something that very few have accomplished. Here are some of the rules for women who are in a committed relationship:

Make sure that you communicate positive, kind, supportive, friendly, empathetic, and compassionate messages to your man far more than critical, negative, angry, judgmental, and unfriendly messages.

Give to your man more than you take. Form the habit of giving, serving, pleasing, and nurturing. You cannot take more than you give, or you risk drying up the reservoir of good will.

Be more fun. Find one or two fun things to do every week that the two of you can do together. Kids can join in, but not all the time. A couple needs some alone adult time to simply enjoy each other's company.

Pick your battles. You're not going to win every argument, so choose your battles wisely and fight for those things that matter the most to you.

During a disagreement, find some truth in what your man is saying—no matter how wrong or misguided you think he might otherwise be. Saying: "You're right. I see where you felt hurt (discounted, railroaded, etc.)" will be far more effective than you arguing, defending, explaining or attacking him for how he feels.

Be physically affectionate every day. Use touch, hugs, kisses, holding hands, caresses, cuddling, and comforting. Physical contact will help him feel closer to you, because he's male—and that's how men tend to feel close to a woman. Touch is no doubt how the two of you got close in the beginning of your relationship, and touch is what will keep your relationship close, connected and intimate today. Affectionate touch is the aphrodisiac that men crave.

Express your love sexually. When women use the word "romance," they're usually referring to love. When men use the word "romance," they're often referring to sex. Sex is central to a man's sense of contentment and his image of his own masculinity. Adopt the attitude: "With my body, I thee worship." If you can't, in good conscience, do that, figure out how to clear up what's in your way.

Learn to be a "student" wife. Most people behave in a marriage the way they think they should, so they quit listening to feedback, requests, lessons, and pleas their partner inevitably offer. In truth, you must learn how to be a good wife, and men don't normally come with a training manual. A "student" wife is a lover in training. She is consistently willing to learn or to take feedback about how she could be better: a better friend, more responsive, more supportive, more romantic. You never "graduate" from this position, by the way, because then you will be less likely to continue trying to be the best wife you can be.

Listen more, talk less.

The heart of whether a man feels valued by you is whether you are responsive to what he says matters the most to him. Therefore, if he says something is important to him, make it important to you if you possibly can.

Let your man know what he does right. Most of us are superb at letting our partners know what they've done wrong.

Ask your man: "Are you getting your needs met in this relationship? If not, what would you like different?"

Tell him what you like and love about him. What character traits does he have that you respect or admire? Is he reliable? Trustworthy? A good father? Is he considerate? Affectionate? Is he fun? Romantic? Good looking? A great dresser? These are the reasons you chose him. Don't keep it a secret. Tell him—or write it in a love letter and give it to him.

There's an art to giving appreciation. Learn that art. Imagine the impact it would have had on you if you grew up in a household where your father thanked your mother for cooking dinner every night or if your mother thanked your father for going to work every day. Try this: go out of your way to thank your partner for what he does for you and for all he has contributed to your life. Spell out what that contribution has been—both the big and the little things—and do this at least once a week from now on.

"It was a woman who drove me to drink–and, you know, I never even thanked her." (W. C. Fields)

MAKING IT SAFE TO BE IN A RELATIONSHIP WITH YOU

Think about the many moments in a relationship when your partner lets down his or her guard and exposes a soft spot. Perhaps it is when he is scrutinizing his bald spot in the mirror and looking forlorn. Perhaps it is when she has removed her make-up and feels less than glamorous. Perhaps it is when he has just finished a painful phone conversation with his ex. Perhaps it is when she is watching a movie and tears start streaming down from her eyes.

When your partner risks being vulnerable in your presence, you can feel very powerful. This quickly becomes a real test of your desire for a healthy partnership. What will you do with that power? Do you insert a little dagger in the soft spot that has just been revealed? Do you use it as an opportunity to assert superiority or to settle an old score? Do you seize that power because it feels good?

All of these are certainly options, but none of them are constructive partnership options.

There is only one constructive option: to make your partner feel safe.

Here are a few things to understand about safety and vulnerability:

- No one can open their heart until they feel safe.
- It takes more courage to be vulnerable than it does to be tough.
- Taking advantage of someone's moment of weakness will never help you build up your own strength or power.
- Provoking jealously to control your partner will lead to your partner's mistrust.
- It's hard for someone to feel loving and close when s/he is also feeling picked on, criticized, or judged. If you have little or no tolerance for differences and find yourself going on the attack, ask yourself: why do these differences make me so angry, so frustrated, so insecure? What fears might be lurking beneath my harsh responses? Why can't I be more accepting?
- Learn to not be threatened by differences.
- Learn to bite your tongue, not your partner.
- Sometimes we get so lost in our own emotional whirlwind that we don't realize how much we are obliterating our partner's feelings. Our terrible sadness trivializes their smaller sadness. Our phobias dominate their smaller fears. Our moods trump their moods. But when partnership is a priority, emotional balance is vital. You have to remind yourself that your partner is entitled to get a little depressed, fearful, anxious, or angry, also. And you have to make room for those feelings, to make it clear that they are welcome.
- Dismantle your emotional land mines, and get a handle on your anger, rage, and reactivity.

- Some of us feel compelled to micromanage our partner's life. We scrutinize their habits, their language, their actions, or their appearance—and provide constant critical feedback. If you need to micromanage something, start by micromanaging your unhealthy impulses, and come to terms with your own control issues. Why do things always have to be your way? Making it safe for your partner to relax and be human means learning to let go of control.

Making the relationship safe means taking responsibility for your own emotions, insecurities, and inadequacies. When we punish our partner for having qualities that are just different from ours, we hurt their spirit—and we hurt the possibilities for a good partnership.

Source: *This Is How Love Works* by Steven Carter (M. Evans Publishing).

"This is the miracle that happens every time to those who really love. The more they give, the more they possess." (Rainer Maria Rilke)

IF YOU LOOK AT WHAT YOU DON'T LIKE, YOU'LL BE UNHAPPY

(So It's Better to Look at What You Do Like)

Dear Neil: Over the past two years, my lady has increasingly gotten on my nerves, and it has made me question whether I want to continue in the relationship with her. In a nutshell, she keeps her apartment cluttered and in great disarray, she talks way too loud (people stare at us in a restaurant), and she has a hard time warming up after we have had a fight.

But she is also a sweetheart: warm, affectionate, and caring, and she has been very good to me. I have every reason to believe she is wild about me. But these annoyances have increasingly gotten under my skin, and I can't let them go. Every time I think about them, they make me upset. She and I have never talked about these issues, because I don't want to hurt her feelings.

So what do I do? It's hard to be around her flaws, but she is also a great person, and I am reluctant to end a relationship with a lady who is so promising. Can you advise me?

—Torn in Vancouver

Dear Torn: You don't want to talk about any of the things you're irritated about because you don't want to hurt her feelings, but you're thinking of leaving the relationship over those issues? Do you think that leaving her will hurt her feelings less than telling her that something is irritating you?

You have a choice. You can either pay attention to (and even magnify) your lady's negative traits and behaviors, or you can appreciate (and even celebrate) her positive qualities and the "gifts" she offers you.

Most of us have faced a similar choice: we either focus on the negative and grow more withdrawn, judgmental, and critical, or we find a way to minimize the things we don't especially like so we can instead focus on appreciating the positive and the hopeful. We can focus on the negative and be unhappy, or we can focus on the positive and feel fortunate, more at peace, and more content.

But in addition to looking at the positives, you must address the irritations you have with her. If you don't address what's bothering you, you will never give yourself the opportunity of repairing what's wrong. You could, for instance, tell her that the disarray and the sloppiness is bothering you, and you don't feel comfortable in her apartment as a result. If she were receptive to your feelings, you could then offer to help her get her apartment in order. Once that happened, you could lavishly compliment her on having such an attractive place, and every time you came over after that, you could tell her how good her apartment looks. In this way, you might help her to defeat the problem—or to greatly reduce her clutter.

Regarding talking too loud, perhaps you could tell her when she's being too loud (she may have deficient hearing, and she may not know that her voice seems loud to you).You might try saying: "Do you know your voice is really loud right now?" or "I'm right here. I can hear you. No need to talk so loud to me." If she is receptive to this feedback, you might be able to help her modulate her voice and make her voice easier on your (and other people's) ears.

Perhaps not every problem can be dealt with and resolved this way, but it sure beats what you're doing, which is building a case against her. Think of being in a court of law, and your lady is on trial. It sure appears as if you have been silently building a case against her, convicting her of her flaws and foibles, and creating a justification in your own mind for leaving her. This means that from time to time, you will look for evidence to support your feelings—in essence looking for things you don't like. But looking at what you don't like will make you unhappy in the relationship, and it's ultimately self-defeating.

If you're not careful, you will talk yourself out of the relationship without ever giving her a chance to address, fix, or correct any of these issues. It is extremely unwise to leave a relationship without ever presenting what's in your way, or what you would need in order to be happy and content with her. She may not do it, but she deserves a chance to know that something's wrong and what she could do if she wanted to fix it.

So again, let me offer you the choice: focus on the negatives (and don't say anything) and be unhappy with her, or focus on the positives (and speak up) and give yourself the opportunity of happily ever after with her. Your call.

"I have never been hurt by what I have not said." (Calvin Coolidge)

MAKE IMPORTANT TO YOU WHAT IS IMPORTANT TO ME

Dear Neil: I have been with my fiancé for over a year now. We are expecting our first child shortly. I moved to his town to be with him, and I just don't like it. The town we are in is very small, and it feels like there are no opportunities here. We are living with his parents, trying to find a place to rent, but nothing has become available. He has a pretty good job, and that's why he says he doesn't want to move, but he isn't looking for or applying for any other job either. I try to talk to him about it, and he just gets upset.

But I am miserable in this small town. I gave up my family, friends, and my work in order to be with him, but he won't do the same for me. Plus, I want to go to college, and that isn't an option here. I don't want to leave without him, but I feel stuck here. What do I do?

—Small Town Nebraska, USA

Dear Small Town: Read the next letter.

Dear Neil: I am in a long-distance relationship with a man in Canada. Recently he made arrangements to talk with me by Skype for the one-year anniversary of my father's death, but his friends came over, and he cancelled me and went out with them. This is not the first time he has let me down in order to be with others. He keeps making plans to Skype with me and then cancels at the last moment. Besides my father dying, I have recently lost both an aunt and an uncle. I also have children who are having issues, and I want him to be there for me.

He says I expect him to be there all the time and that something is always happening to me. But there are moments that I truly need him to be there for me, and he isn't.

—Alone in Lafayette, Indiana

Dear Small Town and Alone: The issue presented in your two letters is ultimately about the request: "Would you make important to you that which is important to me?"

If your partner makes important that which you say is important to you, you will feel loved, cared about, valued, and even cherished. If your partner doesn't do it, or does it for a while and then stops, you won't feel loved, cared about, valued, or heard, and conflict is likely to escalate in your relationship. The two of you will then be in a power struggle: you become increasingly agitated and demanding, and your partner is likely to feel that you're nagging, needy and self-absorbed—so s/he is more inclined to resist you.

The result is often a couple frozen in a cold war with each other. He won't do what's important to you, so you're not going to do what's important to him, either. In fact, you might be tempted to withdraw things he wants and values (affection, sharing, free time, empathy, sex), because you're now hurt, angry, and offended that he didn't honor your needs and feelings. As a couple, your chances of surviving this battle diminish the longer it goes on.

The best way out of this, and sometimes the only way out of this, is to make important to you that which your intimate partner says is important to him or her. To refuse your partner's request is tantamount to telling your partner that s/he isn't important to you, or that his/her wishes, desires or needs just don't matter to you. And that message is overwhelmingly viewed as the kiss of death for most romantic relationships, because to be in a healthy intimate relationship with someone requires that you care about his/her feelings and are responsive to his/her needs.

Of course, it is always possible that one person's needs or wishes are in direct conflict with the other person's. If, for instance, leaving his hometown in Nebraska is something your fiancé is simply unwilling to do, you're going to have to make a hard and sober choice about whether you would be willing to make his small Nebraska town yours, also—and what you would need from him if you were to make that concession. Likewise, if the boyfriend in Canada remains unwilling to consistently be there for you, you're going to have to decide if he is really the right guy for you.

My advice to the two women whose letters are reprinted above: you're going to have to have a very honest conversation with your man, telling him exactly how important your wishes are to you and whether this is a make-it-or-break-it issue for you. If it is, clearly state what it is you require of him in order for you to remain in the relationship and offer concrete steps he can take, along with a deadline for when it needs to happen.

If this isn't a deal-breaker for you, let this issue go, because your man is clearly resistant to it. But be careful of giving yourself up or losing yourself in a relationship in the future, because your needs and wishes matter also, and any man not honoring what you say is important to you is most likely the wrong man for you.

"When you're in love it's the most glorious two-and-a-half days of your life." (Richard Lewis)

STUDENT HUSBAND, STUDENT WIFE

Dear Neil, "I used to think I had no problem with intimacy because I could have sex so easily. I can see now that I used sex as a tool to validate my self-worth. I have been married for fifteen years and have never had any intimacy. Can a forty-two-year-old person learn intimacy?"
—Wanting in Denver

Dear Wanting: We tend to think of a relationship as a destination ("I fell in love, I got married, and I lived happily ever after") rather than a process or a journey ("We're working on improving our communication and how to be more tolerant of our differences"). When we create a relationship, we tend to quit growing and learning about ourselves and our partners.

One skill stands out above all the others if you are wanting to have a close, intimate relationship: the willingness to be a "student" husband and "student" wife. This skill is appropriate whether you have been together for four months or for forty years.

Students don't assume they know what to do. They have the mindset of a beginner ("teach me, I'm open to learning"). The "student" husband/wife does not assume they know how to be a husband or a wife. They're eager to learn, willing to "get it," and are trying to learn the job better. So frequently, people assume they know how to be a wife or a husband, and they quit the process of learning how to be responsive to the other person. They then do marriage the way they think it should be done and quit listening to feedback, requests, and "teachings" their partner inevitably offers.

We all need feedback about what we're doing right and about what we could be doing better, and we need it presented in a gentle enough way so that we can actually hear it.

In truth, nobody knows how to be a good husband or wife to you. They have to be taught what you want, need, and desire so they can learn the job description really well. Being a good student is helped enormously by having a good teacher: someone who is willing to gently teach us how to succeed with them so that we can be spectacularly successful.

Being willing to become a "student" husband or wife is, in my judgment, one of the two keys in being a good husband or wife. Being willing to be an effective and patient teacher is the other key.

That is how this "student" husband tries to go home every night. When I don't, we're often not close. When I do, usually we are. It is a continuous process of "getting it."

Intimacy is about how willing I am to learn how to be responsive and nurturing to someone I care about. I am a specialist on intimate relationships and what goes wrong in intimate relationships, and I have finally figured out that I will never "graduate" and become a husband. A "student" husband is as good as it will ever get. It keeps me tuned in and conscious, and it helps us stay close.

It is easier to get a marriage license than it is to get a driver's license. It is easier to get married than it is to be happily married.

"Romantic love requires courage—the courage to stay vulnerable, to stay open to our feelings to our partner, even when we are temporarily in conflict, even when we are frustrated, hurt, angry—the courage to remain connected with our love, rather than shut down emotionally, even when it is terribly difficult to do so. When a couple lacks this courage and seeks 'safety' from pain in the refuge of withdrawal, as so commonly happens, it is not romantic love that has failed them but they who have failed romantic love."
(Nathaniel Branden)

COMMUNICATING WHEN YOU ARE HURT OR ANGRY

In a fight or argument, what is your fight style? Does one of you run from conflict, refuse to talk about a disagreement, withdraw, cry, shut down, or emotionally disappear in the face of conflict? If so, you fit the description of "conflict avoidance."

Regardless as to the content of what your fights are about, your style of fighting—and your intimate partner's style—speaks volumes about the health of your relationship.

If you are conflict avoidant—or live with someone who is—your relationship is more likely to encounter smokescreens ("what conflict?"), blaming and finger-pointing, sarcastic comments, and frozen anger. All in all, when conflicts get stuffed away, ignored, or avoided, there will be less passion in your relationship, and a lot more distance.

It is true that fighting can damage a relationship, but avoiding conflict is frequently even more destructive. The person who withdraws from conflict or emotionally shuts down harms a relationship because they have cut off all possibility of working out a disagreement. People who disconnect in a conflict bring considerably less to the table in terms of solving a problem or even being able to discuss the problem effectively. They are reacting to a conflict as if their survival is at stake.

There is no way around the fact that if you act self-protective in a disagreement by becoming conflict avoiding, you will lose the feelings of love and closeness and instead become fearful and closed. So an important problem that is unresolved often functions as a small drop of poison to the relationship.

Also, anger that is not expressed openly will still find a way to leak out indirectly, which will further poison the relationship.

If you or your intimate partner are in a relationship that has conflict avoidance, here are some things you could do in order to make your relationship better:

- Quit being so self-protective. It hurts the relationship and isolates you from those you care about. Quit acting as if the conflict is a survival issue unless it genuinely is.

- Write the answers to the following questions on a sheet of paper: I resent … , I'm angry about … , I'm fed up with … , I'm annoyed about … , I can't forgive you for … , I'm hurt by … , I'm suspicious of … , I feel sad when … , I'm disappointed because … , I'm afraid … , I wish … , If only … , I'm worried about … , What I really want is … These questions will give you an idea about what has been troubling you in the relationship.

- Also write the answers to these questions: I appreciate … , I value … , I like … , I feel grateful for … , I forgive you for … , I love … These questions will help you to feel closer. If you think it would be helpful, share these answers with your partner.

- Look carefully at how your anger comes out indirectly, as withdrawal, criticism, sarcasm, rejection, and the like.
- Don't attack your partner or deliver angry personal critiques. Instead, explain what you find distressing about his/her behavior. Start and end the conversation with what's positive about the other person and the relationship.
- Focus on the issue. Edit the hostility or the mean-spirited jab in order to concentrate on the main message. Often the emotional intensity is not meant to be personal, but instead is a signal of the issue's importance.

"The first duty of love is to listen." (Paul Tillich)

QUIZ: ARE YOU SABOTAGING YOUR RELATIONSHIP(S)?

Intentionally or not, might you be sabotaging your intimate relationship(s) with other people? Take this quiz to find out. Rate your answers on a scale from 1 to 5, in which 1 = never; 2 = sometimes; 3 = half the time; 4 = often, and 5 = always. This quiz is courtesy of Randi Gunther in the book *Relationship Saboteurs* (New Harbinger Publications).

1. If you queried all your significant intimate partners, would their complaints be similar?

2. Have you dismissed your partner's requests for change as unimportant?

3. Do you continue with certain patterns of behavior, even when they are clearly driving your partner away?

4. When a partner is distressed with you, do you respond defensively and justify your actions?

5. Did anyone in your childhood justify hurtful behaviors that happened to you or to others?

6. Would you be unable to tolerate a partner behaving the way you behave in your relationships?

7. When you're confronted with behaviors your partner doesn't like, do you try to reverse the blame and focus on your partner's faults instead?

8. Do you expect your partner to excuse your faults because you have good qualities also?

9. Are you likely to blame your partner for behaviors you yourself use?

10. When your relationships have ended, do you typically feel self-righteous and blameless?

11. Are you threatened by your partner's other close relationships?

12. Do you find yourself often seeking reassurance?

13. Do you regularly worry that your partner will leave you?

14. Are you resentful if your partner argues with your decisions?

15. Have past or current partners complained that you dominated the relationship?

16. Can you sometimes allow your partner to tell you what to do?

17. If there is a difference or disagreement, do you insist that things be done your way?

18. If your partner doesn't do what you want, do you punish him/her?

19. Do you find yourself retreating from the relationship when things seem really close?

20. Have you become an expert in convincing your partner to come back after s/he has given up on you?

21. Do you have the pattern of desiring connection but later feel trapped?

22. Do partners tell you that they don't trust your love anymore?

23. When challenged, are you quick to assume a fighting stance?

24. Are you a sore loser?

25. Have past partners complained that, no matter what they do, you didn't believe that they really cared?

26. Does too much happiness make you uncomfortable?

27. Is it hard for you to be interested in someone else's conversation unless it pertains to you?

28. Do you feel neglected when your partner doesn't put you first?

29. Do you have tantrums or withdraw when you don't get your way?

30. Do you verbally dominate conversations?

31. Do you hide your addictive behaviors?

32. Have your relationships fallen apart because of your addictive behaviors?

33. Do you give into behaviors that keep you from being the person you want to be?

34. Do you use name-calling, mud-slinging, silent treatment, withdrawal or threats when you're angry?

35. Are you unable to stop relationship-destructive behaviors even when you know you risk losing your partner?

36. Do you consistently attract selfish or self-centered partners—and then feel used when the relationship is over?

37. If your partner finds fault with something you've done, is your first response to defend yourself?

38. Do you keep your partner from knowing information that would cost you options were s/he to know?

39. Do you do things that betray your partner's trust?

40. Do you take advantage of your partner's gullibility by telling him/her things that aren't true?

Scoring: Add up your total score. A score of 80 and below indicates that although some of your behaviors may be hurtful or annoying, most of the time you're doing what a healthy relationship requires. If you score from 81 to 100, you are distancing from your partner and are at risk of eroding the trust in your relationship. With a score of over 101, you are actively in the process of relationship sabotage.

"Marriage enables a man to find out what kind of man his wife would have preferred." (Janice Casey)

THAT "LOVIN' FEELING" REQUIRES THESE BEHAVIORS

Most of us want to believe the fairy tale we grew up with: that two people can fall in love, get married, and live happily ever after—or some variation of that. Some of us do live that fairy tale, but most of us struggle with the "happily ever after" part. It's not that we don't desire it, but rather that we don't know how to do it, and we certainly don't know how to sustain it over any period of time.

So permit me to offer some suggestions about some of the more important behaviors that are required if you want that lovin' feeling to last into the future:

1. Choose peace over feeling irritated. It's empowering to choose being loving and peaceful instead of responding to an irritation or disappointment with an angry, reactive, or judgmental response.

2. Listen for the longing behind your partner's complaints. You'll hear the important issue that way.

3. Do one thing each day that would help your partner feel more valued, appreciated, or cherished.

4. Good communication requires more than talking. Most people are very good talkers and extremely poor listeners. To listen effectively asks you to hear without defending, explaining, counter-criticizing, or interrupting the other person. (All of those behaviors communicate that I don't value what you are saying, by the way.)

5. I must remove my reactivity, defensiveness, hostility or sarcasm from our dialogues. I must refrain from threatening the relationship, from put-downs, belittling words, nitpicking or being disrespectful. I must learn to express my hurt, anger and frustrations in a more skillful manner, and I must get good at self-editing. No one does well when they feel judged or criticized more than they feel appreciated or respected.

6. Happy couples make their relationship a top priority in their lives. They don't spend their most vital hours consistently preoccupied with other concerns or activities—or too tired.

7. What kind of touch do you want more of? What kind of touch makes you feel closer or more connected? This is a conversation that needs to happen between people who are intimate with each other, because the right kind of touch keeps people closer. It's also appropriate to talk about what kind of touch is unwelcome or does not make you feel closer.

8. Be willing to be the leader in your relationship—the person looking out for the overall welfare of the partnership and of the people within the partnership. That means it's up to me to warm things up between us, to grow the connection and the happiness between us, and I can't take out my negative energy on you.

9. Make sure you do periodic repair work by apologizing when you say or do something that hurts or offends.
10. Pick your battles. You're not going to win every one, so fight only for those things that matter the most.
11. Add surprise and variety so you don't fall into routines that deaden relationship spontaneity and aliveness.

"When a man says, 'We've got to talk,' the woman hears, 'We're going to have a nice conversation.' When a woman says, 'We've got to talk,' a man hears, 'Will the defendant please rise?" (Peter Sasso)

WANT TO FALL IN LOVE? DO THIS

Want to fall in love? Here is a set of questions designed for you to take a promising or hopeful relationship to the next level.

I should state that these questions require someone else's active and willing participation, and it helps enormously if both of you are sexually and/or sensually attracted to each other. Also, both of you must be unencumbered with other romantic attachments so that you are available for a love relationship.

With that in mind, sit facing each other, and look into the other person's eyes as the two of you share your answers to the following questions. Assume there will be multiple answers to each question:

- What assists you in feeling close and connected? What interferes?
- What are the biggest priorities in your life? Where does an intimate relationship fit into these priorities?
- When you become irritable, short-tempered, or hard to be around, what would you like me to say or do? What should I not say or do?

- What are your expectations regarding children, friends, socializing, and partying? How about drug/alcohol use, porn, and opposite-sex friendships? How about ex-spouses or lovers?
- How would you like me to handle you when you're angry? What helps? What doesn't?
- What do you want to accomplish or experience before you die? In the next five years? This next year?
- What are some of the things you're most proud of?
- What are some of the things you're most disappointed in yourself about?
- Describe your best qualities or traits.
- Describe your worst attributes or characteristics. Where do you need to improve the most?
- What do you like about me? About our relationship? About us when we're together?
- If I were to be more open with you about my feelings, I would …
- If I were to be more affectionate and giving toward you, I would …
- When I get withdrawn, you could pull me back by …
- Describe an extremely romantic evening. What does it consist of? What would make this an extremely romantic relationship for you?

- What would help you to feel more cherished, valued, and cared for by me?

Falling in love with someone is both a choice and a decision. It doesn't happen to us—we make it happen, or we block it from happening. It's your decision. Do you want to be in love?

"Want to improve your relationship? See love as a verb rather than a feeling." (Stephen R. Covey)

THE ART OF "STEPPING INTO THE PUDDLE"

Let's say your beloved dog dies and you are heartsick. As you tell different people of your loss, notice your emotional reactions and your gut feelings to the following responses: "I'm sorry for your loss." "You'll get over it in time." "Your dog is in a better place now." "Are you going to get another dog soon?" "It was her time." The reason why none of those responses feel good is that they don't honor your feelings of loss and sorrow. They're not emotionally meaningful replies, and they don't address your feelings at all.

Now notice how you would feel if you were to receive this response: "I am so sorry to hear this news. I would be devastated if my little Fluffy died. Tell me about your dog and your relationship with her. What will you miss about her? It doesn't feel fair that we live so much longer than our dogs, does it? How are you coping?" That reply would feel meaningful, because it actually acknowledges your emotions. It would make us feel closer to the other person, because we feel someone is actually willing to hear our feelings and offer us empathy and compassion.

Authors Pat Love and Steven Stosny call this "stepping into the puddle" in their book *How to Improve Your Marriage without*

Talking about It. Stepping into the puddle involves joining someone with our heartfelt presence, caring concern, and participation. It allows another person to feel that they are not alone in their personal struggles, emotional quandaries, or hurt feelings.

Now imagine if we were really good at doing this at home, especially with our spouses and children. It does not take a large leap to understand that this one relationship skill has the highest potential to transform our important relationships and assist us in feeling closer and more connected to each other.

Why don't more people do this, or do it more often? Largely because they fear they will be stepping into an ocean instead of a puddle—and that they will drown in that ocean of emotion. But that's not how emotions work. It doesn't destroy you because someone else's dog dies. But if you step into the puddle with them, you could help them walk out of that puddle, or walk out of the puddle together with them.

In a relationship, imagine the impact of the following statements: "I'm so proud of you for getting up every morning and going to work, especially when you don't feel like it. You are my hero." "Thank you for putting such effort and energy into making our meals. I feel very nurtured and cared for by you going this far out of your way." "It's amazing that you can work all day and still be such an attentive and loving mother. How do you do it?" "Thank you for being mine. I feel so very lucky for finding you."

That's stepping into the puddle in an entirely different way. It's acknowledging someone's effort or impact on you, instead of their hurt feelings. Is that an ocean you think you would drown in or willingly swim in?

RUNNING AWAY FROM A LOVING RELATIONSHIP

Dear Neil: I've been going out with my boyfriend for six months. He is everything I want in a man, but I keep pushing him away. I'm wondering if it's because of my past. I was physically and sexually abused as a child, and my ex was a bully who was controlling and violent, and I lost my two children to him—so I have a lot of trouble trusting people.

But my boyfriend is everything I want and need in a man. So why am I pushing him away? This man means the world to me, and I don't want to lose him, but I don't know how to fix this. I'm afraid of letting him back in.

—Emotionally Crippled

Dear Neil: My boyfriend frequently backs away from me sexually. Often (not always) we will start making love, and during the act he gets really tired and has to stop. He plays it off to work stress, aging and fatigue. Does this mean he does not want to be close to me? We've been together for a year and a half, and I am the most serious relationship he has had. He is fifty-three and never married. His longest relation-

ship was three years, and he admits that they weren't very close. I am not sure what to do.

—Puzzled

Dear Crippled and Puzzled: Although your stories are different, it appears that the issues you're presenting may be similar. The two of you sound like you're describing a fear of getting close, and one of you may be associating closeness with feeling hurt, controlled, and abused.

This also may be related to feelings of inadequacy and unworthiness, which means that I don't feel worthy of being loved, or I feel that I'm not good enough for you. I fear when you find that out, you're going to eventually leave me, so I wall myself off from you.

The gentleman who is withdrawing sexually may also have performance issues, or he may be simply losing focus or interest—or perhaps his appetite is lower than yours—but it's a good bet he is regulating how close he wants the relationship to become. The woman who is avoiding contact sounds like she is attempting to protect herself from further pain and disappointment, which she assumes is inevitable, and she has become emotionally paralyzed out of fear.

If you're going to fix this, these issues need to be thoroughly laid out on the table and talked about as a couple, so the rejected person knows how to effectively respond, and the relationship is not routinely threatened.

"They say marriages are made in heaven. But so are thunder and lightning." (Clint Eastwood)

WHEN ONE PERSON WITHDRAWS FROM A RELATIONSHIP

Has this happened to you? Two people fall in love with each other. But then one person runs away, pushes the other person away, escalates with anger or personal attacks, or withdraws. The person who has not withdrawn becomes enormously puzzled by this obvious change of heart and frantically attempts to charm, buy, entice, cajole, threaten, or seduce the other person back.

As it turns out, this is a common relationship experience that causes immense heartache and confusion for the person who is being rejected. "What happened?" they ask. This relationship is "The One," so this can't be happening. What can I do to rescue the connection between us? This bond is too important for me to lose.

If the relationship breaks up, there may be many answers to those questions. You may never know with any degree of certainty what actually happened—because the other person may not tell you the actual truth.

What is that truth? The following are some of the more common reasons:

- I didn't actually love you. I tried to, but I couldn't get there—or I got there but I couldn't stay there.

- I'm afraid of being too vulnerable, too exposed, hurt. Intimacy is too close. You could reject me, leave me, or betray me. I can't take that risk, so I run away from love or I push you away. Better to be safe than rejected, abandoned, or found to not be good enough. I'm very afraid you'll find out I'm inadequate and leave me.

- I don't feel worthy of love and/or affection, so I don't let myself love—and I don't give my heart.

- I met someone else I want more than you, but I don't want to hurt your feelings by rejecting you. So I'll make myself very busy or otherwise unavailable, and sooner or later you will get fed up with me and leave me. I don't want you to think I'm the bad guy.

- You were good as a port-in-the-storm, but now I'm looking for someone to be in a serious relationship with, and you don't match my vision of whom I should end up with.

- Actually, I am involved with someone else (or married). But I don't want to get discovered, so I had better cut things off now, before I get caught.

- I won your heart too easily, so something must be wrong with you. You must be needy and desperate for choosing me so readily. So why would I want you?

- I told you what you wanted to hear. I've grown good at acting and pretending.

Some of these answers are cold and callous. Some are completely self-absorbed. Some indicate that I have serious psychological issues. The bottom line is that if it doesn't feel like you are involved with someone who is equally interested in a relationship with you, then probably you're not. Either confront the other person and ask for an immediate change in his/her behavior or drop this relationship and find someone healthy who actually wants you.

"Men build bridges and throw railroads across deserts, and yet they contend successfully that the job of sewing on a button is beyond them. Accordingly, they don't have to sew buttons."
(Heywood Brown)

WHY AM I ATTRACTED TO WITHDRAWN MEN? THE ALLURE OF "UNPREDICTABLE LOVE"

Of the thousands of letters and emails I get from readers around the world asking for relationship advice, the most frequent center around someone in a relationship pushing away or running hot and cold. Here are a few examples:

- My boyfriend and I have been together for a year. After we started living together, he hasn't been as close as he was when we were dating. He doesn't like to cuddle, touch, or be touched. He doesn't like kissing or holding hands, especially in public. We don't even have sex anymore—it's been three months. Finally, he almost never says "I love you." But I know he loves me, because he becomes anxious when we're apart.
- My boyfriend has closed off to me. I make all the effort to make sure he's happy. But I feel I'm always walking on eggshells and constantly filtering what I say so as not to disappoint him. How do I ask him to put in more effort without sounding needy? I'm just too emotionally committed to be the one to leave.

- I was in a relationship with a man for two years, and we only had sex twice. He claimed the issue was with him and didn't want to talk about it. But he left me for another woman, and said our relationship was unhappy because we didn't have sex. He now wants to come back to me. If he doesn't want sex with me, why does he want to be in a relationship with me?

Remember the cartoon character Charlie Brown? He spent his childhood trying to be close to a girl named Lucy, who repeatedly rejected him. He yearned for someone he couldn't have, who was fickle and let him down time after time. Carried into adulthood, many people—men and women—get themselves invested in an intimate partner who becomes detached, who turns hot and cold, who strings you along or who plays hard to get.

Part of this is the allure of "unpredictable love." Unpredictable love offers us novelty, variety, and surprise—something we're not expecting. It's about playing the hard-to-get game and sometimes winning. There's something addictive and exciting about unpredictable love. Many of the men described above thrive on the chase, the challenge of winning you. Once they have you, they may no longer want you, because they're attached to the thrill of the hunt—the excitement of pursuing someone they want—not of actually having you.

My advice: instead of focusing on your man's feelings, focus on your own needs and goals. Give him one warning that you're running out of patience and that you require a change of behavior from him, and if he doesn't respond appropriately, let him go and end the relationship—because you are worth more than this, and you can do better.

The man who is rejecting you may feel entirely differently when he is the one being rejected. If that happens, don't reignite with him quickly if he decides to now be available. Make him prove that he'll commit to you and give you the time, the effort, and the affection you long for. If you don't do that, he'll likely push away again when he is confident he has you back.

"I was dating a transvestite, and my mother said, "Marry him, you'll double your wardrobe." (Joan Rivers)

WHY ARE WE NO LONGER HAVING SEX? WHY RELATIONSHIPS TURN CELIBATE

Dear Neil: My wife and I are married twenty-five years, but we are no longer sexual, and haven't been for three years. I guess you could say we have a celibate marriage, but I don't understand why. We were always frisky with each other, but it slowly lessened until there was nothing at all. Why does this happen, and what can I do about it?

—High and Dry in Denver

Dear Denver: Here are the most common reasons marriages turn celibate:

- Anger or resentment. Hostile, adversarial, or angry energy is likely to turn people off to each other, and as that negative energy builds, people feel hurt and distant from each other, and then they don't want to be loving and giving. Also, the angrier one person gets, the less sexy the other partner is going to feel and the less s/he may want to give to the other.
- At least one person has a low libido, so desire isn't strong, and there is no sense of urgency or hunger. This may be related to

low testosterone (the hormone most closely associated with sex drive) in either partner—male or female, because women have testosterone also, but in considerably lower levels than do men.

- Your relationship has grown cold, disconnected, or distant, where at least one of you no longer feels very close to the other. As that happens, one of you may adopt the attitude that you're not going to give in to the other, or that you don't want to take care of the other.
- The relationship isn't affectionate anymore, and there is very little physical warmth or touch, so sex begins to feel awkward and artificial.
- There are concerns about appearance. Some people no longer feel attractive and therefore don't want to be seen or touched.
- The spark is gone. The relationship is no longer romantic, and therefore there isn't enough erotic build up.
- There is a loss of trust where one person no longer feels safe. A betrayal, an attempted betrayal, or a perceived betrayal all can kill desire and make one person withdraw from the other. A betrayal can also solidify the resolve that you no longer want to give yourself to someone who has treated you badly.
- It can act as protection from feeling vulnerable. If I don't open up to you and allow you close to me physically, then perhaps I won't feel so vulnerable to your judgement, rejection, criticism, withdrawal, or anger.
- Age has a way of humbling many of us. Our minds may be willing, but our bodies may not cooperate. And as we grow

older, we tend to feel tired more of the time—so it can all grow to feel like it's "too much."

- Repetition over time reduces libido. The same thing the same way has a way of growing old and boring.
- Withholding sex can be a way of punishing someone. It can also be used as a form of leverage in negotiating disagreements, conflicts, or issues.
- Illness, surgery or medications: all could repress normal libido or make sex less spontaneous.
- There are medical conditions that can make sex painful or block arousal altogether.
- Some couples don't spend enough time together or do enough activities together for the relationship to feel close and romantic. They may be married, and they may be faithful to each other, but they have grown too far apart, and they have lost the feeling of being friends and companions.
- Because of upbringing, religious teachings or rape or incest, some people grow to feel that sex is wrong, bad, dirty, or demeaning. Using porn, blue movies, fantasies about others or engaging in any sexual activity that the other feels is wrong or distasteful—is also very likely to make your spouse feel bad, dirty, or demeaned.
- There are some people of faith who decide to follow a spiritual path that encourages abstinence.
- It could be that one person hasn't enjoyed sex and therefore has no incentive for engaging in it. One way of helping your

lover to not enjoy the experience is to be too quick, too focused on your own pleasure, or too selfish.

- It may take the two of you so much time, energy, and exertion that it no longer feels worth the effort.
- New parents have so many unusual demands on them—and they often get so little sleep and have so little uninterrupted time alone—that they tend to have much less sex than before. The good news is that this will change, and if you let it, things should go back to normal. Be patient—and take opportunities when they're presented to you.
- Some people have diseases or physical limitations (paraplegia, MS, Parkinson's, etc.) that make them physically unable to perform.

Whatever the reason (or reasons), nothing is going to change unless you invite your wife into a discussion about what has happened and what it will take for the two of you to open up again to each other. If you don't create a dialogue on this subject, nothing is likely to change.

"Men have hidden agendas. For instance, every time a man holds the door open for me, I think he's just doing it to check out my ass. Or at least I hope he is." (Stacey Prussman)

SABOTAGING THE RELATIONSHIP YOU WANT

Do you have a pattern of choosing an emotionally unavailable intimate partner—a person exceedingly difficult to get close to, someone who is emotionally protected, insulated, or standoffish—while rejecting the people who are available, caring, responsive, and easy to be close to?

Do you reject the right person to be emotionally involved with and give everything you have to the wrong person? Do you have a history of sabotaging the intimate relationship you desire?

This pattern typically originates in childhood. If love or approval by at least one of your parents was conditioned on you having to earn it, then you may have grown up feeling that you didn't deserve approval or love unless you had put forth Herculean effort and had proven yourself worthy of it.

So as an adult, if I'm given approval, affection, and love without having to do a lot to earn it, very often I won't value it. I value what I put a lot of effort into, so typically I will chose an intimate partner who isn't prone to offering his/her heart, and then I will do just about anything I can to win his/her acceptance, approval, and love.

If I then enter a relationship with a woman whose heart is easily won over without me having to prove myself, I won't value her, and I won't trust it. It was too easy—so I assume something must be wrong with her. She must be very needy and probably desperate, so I will reject her. But inside I desperately want what she's offering. I want it, but doesn't she know I haven't proven myself worthy of it yet? What's wrong with her? The problem—and this is a big problem—is that I will reject anyone who freely offers me her heart, her love, and her loyalty.

In truth, an intimate partner gives me her heart not because I win it, but because she's ready and able to give it. We don't actually earn anyone else's love, regardless of what you may think. Love is an emotion freely offered, like a gift. It is not possible for me to actually earn your love—you have to make the emotional leap of faith all on your own and give it to me.

So I am sabotaging what I most want, because I'm not giving myself a fighting chance to have what I most desire. In reality, I haven't dealt with the issues that stem from my childhood: I'm afraid of being close, exposed, and vulnerable, and I don't feel worthy of someone else's love and approval.

What could I do to change this pattern? I need to challenge myself to enter a relationship and resist the urge to sabotage it. I need to improve my low self-esteem, so I may eventually feel worthy of someone else's love, and I need to learn how to befriend myself (and offer myself support and guidance) so I'm not so prone to subverting my own goals and desires.

"Ah, women. They make the highs higher and the lows more frequent."
Friedrich Nietzsche

HUSBAND FED UP WITH WIFE'S CELL PHONE ADDICTION

Dear Neil: My wife is beyond obsessed with her iPhone. It is 24/7 with Facebook, video games, and messaging apps, and she clearly prefers her phone to spending time with me and the kids. I assume she is downstairs with the kids, but when I go downstairs the kids are getting into all sorts of things. She is there but not there, immersed in her social media fantasy world. It's ruining our marriage. Even late at night, she would rather play with her phone than be with me. If we didn't have kids, I would have called it quits already.

—Fed Up With Wife's Cell Phone Addiction

Dear Fed Up: Money, sex, trust, children, and poor communication/conflict resolution are still top issues that couple's fight about. But rapidly rising into the mix is the subject you address: feeling ignored or rejected because you do not feel as if you are your spouses/lovers/partner's top priority. And modern electronic devices have become one of the two most common reasons people feel ignored by their intimate partners. (The other reason is work.)

Think for a moment what it would feel like if you're out as a couple sitting in some romantic restaurant or having a serious conversation or the two of you are flirting each other—and your partner gets a text message that s/he feels compelled to respond to right then and there—and this happened over and over again. Most of the time you would feel like the text message took higher priority than you did, and you would feel rejected. Certainly it would kill the mood, but over time it would lead to greater levels of anger, resentment, and feelings of disconnection, because it would feel like casual "friends" are more important to her than you and the kids are.

This may or may not be intentional behavior on your wife's part. That is, she may not be aware of how all of this feels to you. Or on the other hand, she may be avoiding you and intentionally giving you the cold shoulder.

That is where I recommend you start. Tell your wife you need a half hour with her without interruptions after the kids are put down, with her phone off. Then ask her if she's upset or angry with you or if she feels offended by something you've said or done. If she says yes, ask her to talk about it, and be a very good listener. This is no time to explain or defend yourself but to understand her point of view and her feelings. When she is done, ask her what she would need in order for her to fully come back to you.

If she says that nothing's wrong between the two of you and that she is not upset or angry with you, tell her you feel ignored and rejected by her. You can then point out her inattention to you and the kids, and her rapt attention to her cell phone and social media connections.

Recent research on this subject strongly suggests that smartphone/device addiction is associated with depression, anxiety, moodiness, loneliness, stress disorders, and poor engagement at home and work. This may indicate that your wife has a problem that needs to be fixed and that she may not be intentionally ignoring you.

FORGIVENESS REQUIRES LETTING GO OF RESENTMENT

Dear Neil: I wonder if you would address the situation of marital rape. This happened to me many years ago (once). I am a senior now and still have not been able to put this behind me. I still resent my husband deeply, along with his many lies and deceits. He does none of these now, but I believe I should have left him long ago. I still consider leaving him.

—Still Resentful in London, Ontario

Dear Still Resentful: It sounds as if you may be needing to simply talk about what occurred in the past, and the hurt, pain, and anguish that incident has caused you—and that you still feel all these years later. You may also be needing to hear an apology, and perhaps you want him to make some form of amends to you.

But regardless of what your husband does or does not do, you yourself have a big problem, because people who can't let go of their resentment usually become bitter and angry and are in danger of remaining bitter for the rest of their lives. The Buddha identified this dynamic, saying that a person that harbors anger is similar to someone picking up a red hot coal in his/her fingers, getting ready to throw it. You are the one who is more likely to be burned by that coal, not the other person. And in the meantime, it's your quality of life, happiness and spirit that is hurt, not the other person's.

Author Ron Potter-Efron advices us to ask the following questions regarding our resentments: "If you weren't so resentful, how would your life be different? What do you say or do to keep yourself resentful? What thoughts do you have that keep stirring in you? How much of your time has this taken through the years? How much are you ruminating about how burnt you feel? How many of your personal fantasies are related to retribution, punishing, or getting even?"

The solution all this resentment and rumination is to find a way to come to forgiveness. Genuine forgiveness is a shared venture, an exchange between two people, says Janis Abrahms Spring, Ph.D. (www.janisaspring.com) in the book *How Can I Forgive You? The Courage to Forgive, The Freedom Not To* (Perennial Currents). She says genuine forgiveness must be earned, that it comes with a price that your husband must be willing to pay. In exchange, if you're willing, you may eventually allow him to settle his debt. As he works hard to earn forgiveness through genuine, generous acts of repentance and restitution, you work hard to let go of your resentment and need for retribution. "If either one of you fails to do the requisite work, there can be no genuine forgiveness," says Spring. She says both of you need to address the question, "What am I willing to give in order to create a climate in which forgiveness is possible?"

To cut a path to forgiveness, you need to create opportunities for your husband to hear your pain, care about your feelings, and compensate for the harm done to you. If you treat him as evil incarnate and blast him with your silence or rage, you can be sure that nothing corrective will take place, says Spring.

One thing you could do is to let him know what you need from him in order to heal from the incident of the past. In addition, look at how you might forgive yourself for not doing anything about this years ago. If you look carefully, you may discover that the other person you need to forgive is yourself.

It's not too late to resolve your pain, and a couple can grow at any age. But you might have to accept the fact that some injustices will never get settled to your satisfaction. Still, how much longer do you want to be holding that red hot coal in your hand?

"I have never learned anything while I was talking." (Larry King)

LOVE ISN'T ENOUGH

Dear Neil: My fiancé and I are in a fifteen-month relationship, and we're planning on getting married five months from now. But before we marry, we need some help. First of all, you would think that we have been together long enough so that we would have worked out basic living agreements. But no, we focus on very different priorities in our day-to-day lives. He leaves the toilet seat up, leaves his clothes in a pile on the closet floor, leaves dishes in the sink for days at a time, and wants the bedroom window open at night so that we can freeze all night long. All of these just drive me bonkers.

It has gotten so tense between us that we have recently been avoiding each other—going to sleep at different times, eating at different times, and so on. The odd thing about what I'm describing is that I trust that we very much love each other, and we want to marry each other. But we are having a hard time coming to agreement about almost anything right now. Can you help?

—Rattled in Toronto

Dear Toronto: Your letter is a perfect illustration of three "truths" that most people don't understand about intimate relationships. (1) Love isn't enough in order to sustain a relationship. (2) You cannot lose connection with each other, because if you do even small things can grow large. (3) A relationship takes more time, effort, and negotiation than you think it should.

Many people fall in love relatively easily. Some fall in love very easily. Falling in love, although vital, isn't the hard part for most people. It's living together afterwards that's hard.

It's doing the hard work of a relationship: blending, compromising, being kind and gracious even when you don't feel like it, giving in at times, picking your battles, being empathetic, reaching out, apologizing, considering the other person's wants and needs to be equal to your own, occasionally bending to someone else's will—these constitute the hard work of a relationship, and they are often not fun—and certainly not sexy.

The central dilemma you describe is that you and your fiancé are having a hard time resolving your differences so that the relationship can grow and progress. Because you have been unable to resolve those differences, the two of you are in a standoff that is threatening to derail the relationship and sever the connection.

The solution to your dilemma is to reestablish the connection the two of you obviously once had. You're telling me about the differences, but there is perhaps more power in looking at the similarities right now, including your common interests; your long-range goals together; what you like, appreciate, admire, and love about each other; what attracted you to each other; what you like about the relationship; and where your hopes lie regarding the future of the relationship. Those are what connect you to each other, and you cannot afford to lose that connection again in the future. Ways to reconnect include affectionate touch and someone calling even a temporary truce to the power struggle the two of you are currently in.

The third problem you've presented is that you expect to be finished with the blending process that takes years for many couples, if not decades. And you want it all finished and resolved right now, which is understandable but perhaps not realistic. To get solid and feel compatible, a relationship takes way more time than you think it should. Living with someone else is hard. You have different habits, different ways of feeling comfortable at home, different tastes, a different sense of style, different values about what's truly important—of course you're going to have growing pains when you try to live as one.

Sit down with your fiancé, call a truce to the hostilities, and find ways of reconnecting.

And welcome to marriage.

"We have a picture of the perfect partner, but we marry an imperfect person. Then we have two options. Tear up the picture and accept the person, or tear up the person and accept the picture."
(J. Grant Howard, Jr., Journal of Psychology and Theology.)

SELF-CARE: THE ART OF NURTURING YOUR BODY, MIND, AND SPIRIT

Perhaps it starts with you losing your sense of engagement with your work, your children, or your vital relationships. Perhaps it is because you have too many distractions—increasingly electronic postings, emails, texts, or phone calls. Perhaps it is because you have too many demands and responsibilities, and not enough time to do everything you need to do. Or maybe you are doing too many things that feel trivial or lacking in importance.

The next thing you know, you're feeling listless, demoralized, depressed, or burned out. Your work performance declines, your personal relationships begin to grow disconnected, and you feel increasingly dissatisfied with your life. Your involvement and enthusiasm recedes, you feel less alive, and you quit caring about people and activities that used to matter to you.

If this describes you even some of the time, you are suffering from symptoms of burnout—which means you are not doing enough self-care activities that replenish your mind, body, spirit, life goals, desires, and hopes.

Self-care activities are the actions we take that give meaning to our lives or that further our long-term goals or that feel reinvigorating, energizing, or exciting. And they're different for each of us. You might find a day at the beach restorative, where I may need to travel to someplace new. A hike in nature may regenerate you, whereas I may need to go camping and canoeing. None are bad choices, but some will speak more loudly to you than they will to me.

Here are some things you can do in order to create self-care activities that speak to you. First, you could take a break in your day every sixty to ninety minutes to do something refreshing for ten minutes, such as walking around the block, meditating, or listening to music that energizes you. Second, you could plan a luncheon with someone you'd like to be with. Third, set aside at least one hour a week to reflect on your short, medium, and longer range goals—so you're not just doing what is urgent, but also what will feed your soul, spirit, and long-term dreams.

Fourth, always have something in front of you that you're looking forward to doing (taking a road trip, reading a novel, completing a house project that you've never gotten around to, planning a visit with close friends or relatives, going to a bed and breakfast for a weekend getaway). Fifth, how about adding romance to your relationship this weekend?

Make some time—even small amounts of time—to do things that you find energizing or exciting. Find something to look forward to this week, this month, and next month. And limit the amount of electronic distractions that you allow. They don't feed you—they deplete you.

HOW DO I BECOME SELF-LOVING?

Dear Neil: I'm fifty-four and have had to face aloneness, fear, and memories of childhood rape and emotional abuse. How do I become self-loving?

—Trying to Heal, Wellington, New Zealand

Dear Trying: You don't have control over how you grew up, which is where we form our original self-image and where our lack of self-esteem and self-love are created.

But you're now an adult, and you have the power to partly redo your self-image. Self-love is about being on your own side, believing in yourself and being friendly to yourself and what happens to you. It is about feeling worthy of achievement, friendship, love, and respect.

In order to love yourself, you need to focus on what you admire and respect about yourself rather than looking at all the negative traits you think you have. What do you like about yourself? What are your strengths as a person? A friend? A lover? A spouse? A family member? A parent? At work? At home? Socially?

What are the gifts, talents, skills, and good qualities you have? Where in life do you conduct yourself with honor and integrity? When have you risen to the occasion, helped other people out, done the right thing? What traits do you have that you admire and respect when you see them in others? What skills and abilities do you possess that are valuable in helping you cope with the challenges life forces on you?

Figure out what your life's goals are and go after achieving those goals. Loving yourself is about you being on your side, and it does not require you being against anyone else. It requires your care, concern, and friendliness about what happens to you, as well as what you feel and think. It is rejecting to be an opponent or a combatant to yourself. More than just a feeling, loving yourself is about making a conscious decision to be your own best friend.

These are the first steps to loving yourself, and they are necessary before you're going to feel worthy of someone else's love.

"No one can make you feel inferior without your consent."
(Eleanor Roosevelt)

SELF-LOVE REQUIRES BEING ON YOUR SIDE

When you love and value yourself, you start taking care of your health, your body, your psyche, your relationships with others, and your overall well-being.

Here are some of the things you can do to better love, respect, and value yourself:

- Reach out to new people. Continuously expand your circle of friends and acquaintances.
- Go after creating your highest goals and visions. Quit wishing they will just happen on their own.
- Take more risks.
- Become more a participant in life and less an observer.
- Figure out how to play more and have more fun, and do so on a regular, ongoing basis.
- Quit wasting time on things that do not serve your best interests.
- Regularly rise to the occasion and do what needs to be done.

- Let hope run your life, not fear.
- Put out more positive energy—and act more optimistic and hopeful.
- Take overall better care of yourself. Nurture yourself in positive, life affirming, and healthy ways.
- Be in touch with your heart and spirit on a daily basis.
- Quit doing things that hurt you and/or other people.
- Face and deal with your guilt, shame, fear, self-blame, low trust, anger, depression, and other negative emotions—until you defeat them or get them under your control. Don't take these emotions out on other people. You'll feel worse about yourself if you do, and you'll injure your relationships with others.
- Act with integrity and honor in your dealings with others.
- Don't watch too much TV, drink, eat or work too much, or excessively indulge your negative habits or destructive addictions.
- Live consciously. Ask yourself: Am I using my life in a valuable way? Am I enhancing myself and my life by how I am spending my time and energy? Am I using my talents and abilities? How could I better use them? What do I need to do differently in order for the next twenty years to be better than the previous twenty years?
- Are there any dreams that you want to attain that you're not going after, or that you're going after passively? Not going after and trying to create what you want for your life is how we wind up full of regrets.

- Keep your relationships with other people healthy—and treat the people close to you as if you truly value them.
- Train yourself to be appreciative of your life every day. What are you most grateful or appreciative of today? This month? This year? Last year? The last five years? The last ten years?
- What could you do to improve your health, body, and level of fitness?
- What or whom do you still have to forgive?
- What experiences, accomplishments, or achievements are you proud of? Which have added meaning and value to your life?
- What adventures do you want in your future? What are you doing to make those adventures attainable?
- Tend to your sexual health and well-being.
- While you're alive, make sure you're living.

"To most people I'm nobody. But what matters is being somebody to everybody who's somebody to me." (Ashleigh Brilliant)

DOES A LONG-TERM EXCLUSIVE RELATIONSHIP DEADEN SEXUAL DESIRE?

Does a long-term exclusive relationship deaden sexual desire? Does being with the same sexual partner year in and year out lead to feelings of monotony? Do closeness and intimacy lead to good sex, or do people have the best sex during dating, courtship, and/or early marriage?

Perhaps you have some experience that no matter how hot your relationship begins, and no matter how much action the two of you used to have, sexual charge very often peters out over time. It could be that she is tired or angry. It could be that he has lost the interest he used to have, but it could also be that he has been rejected enough that he no longer tries. It could be that romance has fizzled through the years, but it also could be that the two of you have lost the close connection you once had.

Do we grow bored by having sex with the same person over time? Does sameness lead to routineness, repetitiveness, tedium, and feeling mechanical? And is there anything we can reasonably do about this?

Actually, there is. Eroticism is indeed numbed by repetition—so that's where you could start. By adding novelty, adventure, and stimulation to your relationship, which may include the bedroom, but don't limit it to that one arena. Where else in your relationship could you add adventure and novelty? By traveling to someplace new, taking a dance class together, learning a foreign language? By spending twenty minutes every night talking about your hurts, hopes, and dreams? By buying a book with different sexual positions and making an agreement to try every last one of them?

Foreplay does not begin a few minutes before the main event; it starts at the previous erotic encounter. Way too many people make the fatal mistake of putting the minimum amount of effort and energy into romance, having fun together, going out on dates, talking intimately, and being a friend. But adult sex that stays interesting and titillating requires continuous effort and energy—it requires you to live as lovers, not just as husband and wife.

What do you do to fan the flames of romance in your relationship, and how often do you do it? Would your spouse or lover say that you live as a sweetheart, or are you sweet when you want sex? Would your partner say you are more complimentary or critical? Are you angry a lot? What do you do to restore or enhance the connection with your lover, and how often do you do it?

How often are you putting forth real effort in listening to your spouse about his fears about money or what's concerning him at work? How frequently are you willing to lovingly attend to her emotions? What are you doing to keep romance alive on a day-to-day basis? How often are you erotically playful with your partner—I'm thinking of lingerie, weekend getaways, naughty voicemail messages, sitting holding hands while you talk, cuddling, and so on.

If you want your relationship to be more erotically charged, go make it happen. And quit waiting for it to happen.

SUGGESTIONS FOR A MORE ROMANTIC RELATIONSHIP PART 1

Underneath all our differences, men and women both want the same things: to be loved, cared for, respected, appreciated, and desired. We all want a place of safety and security where we can be ourselves, and where we can grow and mature. And we all want our intimate relationship to be outrageously romantic. I certainly do. Don't you?

Imagine how you would feel if, in the middle of a party or other social event, your spouse or intimate partner turned to you and said "I can't imagine my life without you in it." Or if he said "I'm glad I married you." Imagine playing footsies under the table in an elegant restaurant, charging him twenty kisses for making dinner—or for him taking your car in and getting your tires rotated. Or imagine him kissing your hand like you were British royalty. Or if she ran her hands under hot water before she joined you in bed.

Those are called romantic gestures, and they are one of the things that will put a bounce in your step and make you feel intoxicated with warm, loving, intimate, and lustful feelings. Here are "secrets" for how to turn your relationship into a love affair all over again, courtesy of Gregory J. P. Godek in his book *1001 Ways to Be Romantic* (Sourcebooks Publishers, 2010):

- Learn what she likes/wants. Get it for her, but hold onto it for several weeks (or months).This gives her time to forget about it or to think you have forgotten. Surprise her with it when she least expects it. And don't give practical items (such as a toaster oven or sweatshirt) as a gift for any romantic occasion.

- Call your lover on the phone. Make up a love song on the spot and sing it to her. Make up the words and the tune—and just keep singing. It doesn't have to make any sense, and you don't have to be musically talented. You'll generate laughter as well as appreciation.

- Write reminders to yourself in your calendar or smart phone—two weeks in advance of her birthday, anniversary, and any other important occasion—so important dates don't sneak up on you. You can then be prepared to send a card, buy a gift, or make a reservation.

- Doesn't he deserve a trophy for being the "World's Best Lover" or for getting a promotion at work or for coaching the boys basketball league or for being a loving and involved dad? Or you could create a custom certificate "For Putting Up with Me over the Years," or for "The World's Best Husband." Trophy shops have a wealth of ideas waiting for you. Just think of the romantic possibilities of plaques, ribbons, nameplates, certificates, and banners. All of them can be personalized, engraved, lettered, or monogrammed.

- Gift-wrap your gifts. Remember that the presentation is almost as important as the gift itself. You do a great disservice to yourself and your relationship when you're too casual about how you offer your gifts and presents. Nicely wrapped gifts have twice the impact as those that are poorly presented.

- Do you know what your partner finds erotic? Are you sure you know? Here's something you might try: talk about what each of you considers to be erotic and sexy. Be open to new and different ways of erotic expression.

- Go hiking. Go tobogganing. Go to a ballgame. Go to a park. Go for a drive in the country. Go to a public garden. Go to an outdoor concert. Go on a picnic. Go for a walk. Go fly a kite, share a board game, play cards, or toss a Frisbee. Make sure you're not letting your life together get stale or boring.

- Whisper sweet nothings in her ear while out in public. Or try whispering shocking comments and lewd suggestions to her at a more formal gathering. That should add a little spark for the evening!

- Romantics are always "dating." In fact, regularly going out on dates is every bit as important for long-married couples as it is for people who are just getting to know each other.

- Advice for single guys: How to catch her: learn to dance. How to keep her: learn to cook.

- Make a toast to one another every time you hold a wine glass. Make eye contact. Take turns making the toast.

- Write your own words of love. Some ideas: Reasons I Fell in Love with You; Reasons I Still Love You; Ways You Turn Me

On; Things I Look Forward to with You; Things I Admire or Respect about You, or write your own version of Elizabeth Barrett Browning's famous sonnet, "How do I love thee? Let me count the ways."

"Any man who can drive safely while kissing a pretty girl is simply not giving the kiss the attention it deserves. (Albert Einstein)

SUGGESTIONS FOR A MORE ROMANTIC RELATIONSHIP PART 2

No adult reading this article is likely to be a novice when it comes to romance. Most of us have been around the block once or twice when it comes to our experiences in an intimate relationship, and some of us have been around the block over and over again. We all know the pattern. Two people fall in love. They do all the classic romantic things that couples do when they first get together. But, over time, the passion and romance fade—sometimes never to return. Some would argue that this is inevitable in a relationship.

But passion does not need to fade in your relationship any longer, and "generic romance" will take you only so far. A relationship between once-close lovers will drift apart if both of you don't work at keeping things close, connected, and loving on an ongoing basis. Familiarity does not "breed contempt," but boredom, lack of effort and lack of initiative will. You just need more creative and personal ways of living your love, because while falling in love just happens, staying in love never happens by itself.

"Great relationships aren't 50/50. They're 100/100," says Gregory J.P. Godek in his book *1001 Ways to Be Romantic* (Sourcebooks Publishers, 2010). "Fifty-fifty really means "I'll meet you halfway." Love is about giving 100%, not merely 50% ....The problem is when you're both trying to limit your giving to your "fair share"—usually defined as 50%. If you do that, you'll definitely fall short of 100%."

Here are some "secrets" Godek offers in how to turn your relationship into a love affair all over again:

- Give your relationship the top priority in your life (and your time and effort are far more important than the money you spend). Gifts are great, but nothing makes up for lost time or for feeling lonely while in a relationship. Make sure you're carving time out of your evenings and weekends to spend with your sweetheart.
- Once a week for a year, jot down two reasons why you love him/her, one great thing s/he did, and one inspirational thought that feels significant to you. At the end of the year, print all of this out on a big scroll and present it to your lover.
- Not for newlyweds only: every so often, carry her over the threshold of your house or apartment.
- Remove yourself from the electronic and media grid on a regular basis—over a weekend, on a vacation, and on random days. In order to slow down and connect one on one with your lover, it helps immensely if you occasionally disconnect from the Internet and email, from TV and radio, from newspapers, magazines, cable, videos, mobile phones—and from the media in all its forms.

- Call from work simply to say "I love you!" (There's rarely an acceptable reason to go eight straight hours without touching base.)

- When women use to the word "romance," they're usually referring to love. When men use the word "romance," they're often referring to sex. So if you want to be really romantic to your lover, be romantic the way s/he defines romance, not the way you do.

- Fill up an entire packet of Post-It notes with twenty-five sexy messages, sixteen romantic suggestions, thirty-one silly notes, seven romantic song lyrics, twelve suggestive messages, and nine intriguing questions. Stick up two notes per day where they will be seen, until you use up the packet.

- How about staging a personal Lingerie Fashion Show for him? Or gals, perform a personal striptease for him. Some stripteases emphasize the strip part, while others emphasize the tease part. You choose.

- When was the last time you told that special someone how lucky you felt to have her in your life? Complimenting her in front of someone else will make her feel extra special.

"Men are from Earth. Women are from Earth. Deal with it."
(George Carlin)

SEXUAL "SECRETS" EVERY WOMAN SHOULD KNOW

If you ask a room full of grown women what they think about men and sex, you are likely to get an earful. Many women complain about men—and their sexual behaviors and attitudes. You will hear women talk about men being too fast, about the lack of prolonged foreplay, about not being kissed enough or not being kissed well enough, the lack of sustained romance in a long-term relationship, and about men being sexually selfish.

Of course, some of this criticism is well deserved. A man may be guilty of some or all of the above offenses.

However, what you're extremely unlikely to hear is women talking about how to be better lovers themselves. Here are some recommendations if you as a woman desire to learn how to be a better lover yourself:

- Accept the fact that he's male—and that means that sex is central to his feelings of contentment and his image of his own masculinity. Give sexuality a high priority in your relationship no matter how busy or preoccupied your life is. Author Michele Weiner-Davis, (www.divorcebusting.com) in her book *The Sex-Starved Marriage* (Simon & Schuster) reminds women that a man's self-confidence and feelings of well-being hinges on lovemaking more than you'd ever guess.

- When men are asked about how the sexual experience could be improved, they routinely report that they would like the woman to initiate more often. Here are several ways how: make eye contact with him, and while he is watching take off every stitch of your clothing; create a sexy voice by adding a breathy sound to it, punctuating your words with more air. Or embrace him, look him in the eye and then say: "I want you now."

- It is arousing to a man when you're aroused. That is, your arousal stimulates his arousal. So what arouses you? Tell him—and then guide him to learn it well.

- Teach your man to kiss you the way you long to be kissed—by letting him know that it's the gateway to greater glories. Author Sallie Foley suggests that you tell him there's something you'd like to show him, and then kiss him exactly the way you would like him to kiss you. Then ask him to repeat the kiss right back to you. Do this as often as you would like. If he does it, show him how much you love it.

- Talk in sensuous ways that author Bonnie Gabriel terms "verbal foreplay." Use your words to ignite his erotic imagination and build a provocative mood of expectation and suspense. Tell him how hot he is, how sexy he makes you feel, that you want to be touched by him, that you can't wait to get him into bed and to pleasure every molecule of his being. Your words can be used as aphrodisiacs. Use them that way.

- If your appetite isn't as strong as his, every so often be willing to "take care" of him all the same. You can't do this a lot or you will grow angry and resentful, but doing this occasionally is wonderfully loving and caring.

- "Many men don't get the same charge out of talking that women do. Your man wants to feel connected to you, but for him your physical relationship—rather than your verbal relationship—is the tie that binds. Physical contact makes him feel closer to you," says author Michele Weiner-Davis. She further asserts that once a man feels close "man style," he's more motivated to meet your need to talk, spend quality time together, and get close "woman style."

- Initiate a conversation about lovemaking, including romance, mood, environment, frequency, foreplay, intercourse, and after play. Ask him to speak to the following sentences: "I really enjoy/appreciate it when…" "I'm uncomfortable about …" "I'd like to …" "I'd like you to …" After you listen to him, then it's your turn to answer the same questions. In this way, the two of you can decide if there are behaviors you'd like to change, try, or experiment with.

- Ask him what romance means to him, and ask him to describe what a very romantic experience is—and give it to him if you can. Then tell him what feels romantic to you. If he does what you describe, show him how much you like it.

- Ask yourself how you could be 5 percent more effective as a friend, companion, and lover to your man. I'm asking you to look at how you could single-handedly be more responsive to your man's needs, and assist him in feeling more cherished by you. Learn the power of doing 5 percent more. Its value is way, way more than 5 percent.

"See, the problem is that God gives men a brain and a penis, and only enough blood to run one at a time." (Robin Williams)

THE STORE WHERE YOU CAN CHOOSE A HUSBAND

There is a new store in New York City where women can go to choose a husband. This is how the store operates:

- You may visit the store only once. You may not come back.
- There are six floors, and the attributes of the men increase as you climb floors.
- But there's a catch: you can choose a man from any floor, or you may go up a floor, but you can't go down.

So a woman goes to the Husband Store to find a husband. On the first floor is a sign: "These men have jobs."

She goes to the second floor and sees a sign: "These men have jobs and love kids."

On the third floor the sign says: "These men have jobs, love kids, and are extremely good looking."

Wow. She's tempted.

But she goes on to the fourth floor: "These men have jobs,

love kids, are drop-dead gorgeous, and help with the housework."

Now she's really, really tempted.

But eventually curiosity gets the best of her, and she goes up to the fifth floor: "These men have jobs, love kids, are drop-dead gorgeous, help with the housework, and have a strong romantic streak."

She waivers. That's exactly what she has been looking for.

But she can't stand not knowing, and therefore she goes up to the sixth floor. The sign says: "You are visitor 31,406,388. There are no men on this floor. This floor exists solely for the purpose of proving that women are impossible to please."

—Anonymous

"The male ... believes that having sex is the central biological reason for his existence. All guys do. We guys get accused of just wanting to get laid a lot, but the truth is that we have been entrusted with an extremely important responsibility—the very survival of the species—and by gosh we're going to try to carry out this responsibility, even if it means we have to try to have a lot of sex. Don't thank us. We're just doing our job." (Dave Barry)

WOOING

Ah, springtime. The time when nature wakes up again. Birds migrate. Plants burst out of the ground with a profusion of green everywhere. Flowers bloom. Fish spawn. Animals breed. All of nature comes alive.

Including us. And the way many of us express that aliveness is through urges of desire and yearning—expressed as wooing.

What is wooing? Wooing can be divided into three categories: 1. Bad wooing 2. Good wooing 3. World-class wooing.

Bad wooing needs no introduction—everyone past the age of twelve has had some experience with bad wooing. (Just kidding. It's probably thirteen.) You know someone is paying attention or flirting with you, but s/he is doing it so subtly, dispassionately, incompetently, or half-heartedly, you don't feel enticed by it. Bad wooing doesn't leave you feeling special, valued, seduced, or summoned.

Good wooing does.

Good wooing involves: lots of time, attention, and energy; presence; increasing levels of curiosity about each other; lots of eye contact; openness to being influenced by each other's ways of looking at things or doing things; being an active and involved listener;

making plans for interesting and/or fun things you can do in the future; genuine compliments or flattery (nothing false allowed); creating lots of opportunities for future invites; accommodating to each other's likes, preferences, tastes, interests, and range of emotions; putting serious effort into deepening the relationship; being responsive to the other person's efforts; being romantic through word, deed, and touch; and showing, not hiding, your interest in the other person.

Wow! What could be better than that?

Well, that's where world-class wooing comes in.

World-class wooing combines all the traits of good wooing and then adds the emotional dimension: being emotionally open; wanting to share your inner self; wanting to truly know the other person (and be truly known by the other person); blending your wishes, hopes, and dreams with the other person's; and being team players by creating a working partnership.

This requires that I communicate that I want to be with you: that I view my life being better off with you than without you, that your presence and your spirit enriches my life and adds value and meaning to my world.

Wooing is a two-person adventure involving a "can-do" attitude, being receptive to the other person—and to the possibilities we could have together as a couple. It involves active, not passive effort.

Which one of the three wooing categories fits you and your style right now? Which one of those categories would you like to fit?

If there is a discrepancy between your current style and your ideal style, what could you do about that discrepancy?

"You can tell you're in love by the way you feel. Your head becomes light, your heart leaps within you, you feel like you're walking on air, and the whole world seems like a wonderful and happy place. Unfortunately, these are also the four warning signs of colon disease. So it's always a good idea to check with your doctor." (Dave Berry)

THE CURE-ALL FOR DISCONNECTION:
The Only Connection Skill You Are Likely to Need

Dear Neil: Can you help me repair my relationship? My sweetheart and I have lost the ability to be close with each other. Here's how a typical conversation between us goes: Me: "How was your day?" Her: "I'm annoyed. I feel like I'm a verbal punching bag at work. I'm in a bad mood." Me: "Well you're not at work now. Let's do something fun." Her: "You do it. I don't want to do anything tonight."

I know she is disturbed by things not going well at work, but she won't let me bring her out of her funk, and she's almost always in a miserable frame of mind, so it's very unpleasant to be around her for any length of time. Any suggestions as to what I can do?

—Feeling Disconnected in Denver

Dear Feeling Disconnected: Perhaps the only real connection skill is to be able to "step inside the puddle" with someone else.

"Stepping into the puddle" refers to conscious emotional attunement to another person, meaning you have to temporarily stop focusing on your feelings or needs and instead tune into how your mate is feeling. That will assist you to feel the emotions, fears and anxieties she's feeling.

Stepping into the puddle asks you to temporarily let go of your judgments and wishes in order to be more emotionally aligned with your partner's feelings or concerns. It's about temporarily joining your sweetheart with your presence, your response, your touch, and your heartfelt participation: "I'm sorry to hear that." "That must feel terrible." "That sounds exciting." "I'm so proud of you." "You give so much, no wonder you're exhausted." "I can only imagine how I would have handled that." "Did that make you anxious?"

Joining someone with your presence and your participation is not a bottomless pit of despair. It's a puddle, not an ocean you're stepping into, and it's designed to help the two of you connect and feel close with each other. Your willingness to step into that puddle with her will also help her to feel safe around you, as if you are one of her close natural allies and friends.

Granted, you have to be able to look past your resentments, your disappointments, your grievances, and your urge to withdraw. But when you allow yourself to feel what she is feeling, you'll likely find that your willingness to join in her emotions will not drag you down but rather assist the two of you in walking out of the puddle together.

This idea comes from Patricia Love (www.patlove.com) and Steven Stosny (www.compassionpower.com) in their book *How to Improve Your Marriage without Talking about It* (Broadway Books). This process is greatly aided by affectionate touch and direct eye-to-eye contact whenever possible, along with hugs, holding her hand, putting your arm around her, and neck massages, to name a few.

Here's how it might work if you were to step into the puddle with your sweetheart: You: "How was your day?" Her: "I'm annoyed. I feel like I'm a verbal punching bag at work. I'm in a bad mood." You: "Would you like to talk about what happened at work today?" Her: "I don't feel respected at all. After three years I'm still treated as if I'm a beginner that needs to be told what to do. I feel insulted all day. It's humiliating." You: "I'm so sorry, honey. That must really be painful to go through. I can't imagine how that must feel. I'm sure that would offend me, also." Her: "Yeah, it put me in a bad mood." You: "No wonder you feel awful. What would ease your pain and help you to feel better?" Her: "Would you give me a back rub?" You: "I'd be happy to do that."

"If a woman has to choose between catching a fly ball and saving an infant's life, she will choose to save the infant's life without even considering if there are men on base." (Dave Barry)

COUPLE'S COMMUNICATION EXERCISE

With couples who enter marriage therapy complaining of communication problems, I sometimes offer them communication skill-building exercises as a way for them to talk more openly with each other. One such exercise follows, courtesy of Jennifer Louden in *"The Couples Comfort Book"* (Harpers San Francisco)(www.jenniferlouden.com):

- When I think of nurturing the relationship, I think of …
- When I think of intimacy, I think of …
- When I think of tenderness, I think of …
- When I think of commitment, I think of …
- When I think of sacrifice, I think of …
- I feel loved and nurtured when you …
- You could help me talk about my feelings more by …
- If I were able to be more open about my feelings …

- If I were to be more open about your feelings …
- I've noticed recently about myself …
- I am a person who needs …
- To nurture and take care of myself more, I need to …
- When I take time just for me, I feel …
- When I take time just for me, I think you feel …
- One of the things I admire about you is …
- One of the things you taught me is …
- One of the things you're really good at is …
- If I could change one thing about our relationship, it would be …
- If you really loved me, you would …
- One of your strengths that balances me is …
- When I was growing up, I learned that sex was …
- One of my fondest sexual memories with you is …
- To feel "in the mood" I need …
- If you could do one thing different next time we make love, I would like you to …
- One of the ways I block love is to …
- One of my fondest memories of you is …

- One of my fondest memories of us is …
- The most important decisions we need to make together are …
- The most important issues or conflict we need to resolve or get better at are …
- I would really like it if you would …

Be sure you are face to face, have eye contact, and there are no distractions such as TV or children. Let each person answer each question thoroughly, which means there will be multiple answers to each question. No interrupting.

"Men won't stop and ask for directions because driving is too much like sex: they can't stop until they get where they're going."
(Diana Jordan)

TRAITS OF HAPPY COUPLES

What can you do to create the best relationship possible—a close, intimate, happy, heartfelt, soulful, romantic, connected, affectionate, and passionate relationship?

I am talking about creating—not simply having—the best relationship possible, because while falling in love just happens, staying in love never happens by itself.

We begin our relationships full of hope and promise, vowing to give our best. Isn't it sad that so many people who start out with close, exciting, erotic relationships find themselves just a few years later with angry, distant, withdrawn, and passionless relationships?

Nobody has a perfect relationship all the time. Even the best, most perfectly matched couples have hard times, misunderstandings, and heated arguments.

But the best relationships do not allow themselves to be so overwhelmed by daily concerns, work, moods, irritations, grievances, disappointments, or resentments that their dealings with each other become angry, detached, withdrawn, and lacking in spirit.

So how do you achieve and maintain the best relationship possible?

Here are the behaviors and traits of happy couples:

- **They are affectionate with each other,** and both parties are happy with the degree and frequency of affection. Happy couples touch each other a lot. They have learned how to offer caresses, affection, and cuddling.
- **They share their feelings with each other.** Emotions are solicited, accepted, received well, and tended to—and are treated with friendliness, empathy, compassion, and kindness. Each partner's feelings are given a respectful hearing and are treated as important.
- **They are both good listeners.** Both feel as if their voices are heard and honored by the other. Neither interrupts or cuts the other off when attempting to express him/herself.
- **Happy couples function as each other's emotional support system in times of distress or crisis.** They're friendly to each other's concerns and struggles.
- **Each partner is in control of his/her negative emotions,** such as anger, hurt, jealousy, insecurity, fear, and anxiety. That means I do not take out the frustration, anger, or hurt I have about other things out on you, and you need not fear that you will be the main recipient of my negative energy, hostility, argumentativeness, disrespect, or anger.
- **Happy couples spend time together and tend to do things with each other.** They prefer to be in each other's company most of the time. They make their intimate relationship a top priority in their lives. They don't spend their "prime time" too tired or preoccupied with other things.

- **Happy couples treat each other well** with kindness, good spirit, and benevolence. I treat you like I truly cherish you.
- **There is a sense of true partnership between equals.** Major decisions (and many of the minor ones) are made jointly. Both feel the division of labor is more or less fair as it relates to roles, chores, and housework.
- **They have made peace with past hurts with each other,** by talking about, working through, and resolving past wounds, disappointments or breeches of trust. Heartfelt apologies have been extended for previous hurts and grievances so that forgiveness can be genuinely and cleanly offered back.
- **Happy couples have learned how to have fun together** on a regular and ongoing basis.
- **There's an attitude of unselfishness.** Looking out at the world binocularly rather than monocularly. Your needs, wants, feelings, and preferences are treated equally to mine.
- **They trust each other.** They give their mate the benefit of the doubt with an assumption of good will and good spirit. Anything in the way of either party trusting the other fully gets cleared up immediately.
- **They keep sight of the long term,** and therefore don't threaten each other's sense of long-term security or stability. Neither threatens the future of the relationship or uses such threats as bargaining devices.
- **They value romance.** Wooing, sweet gestures, special meals, help around the house, surprises, flowers, notes and cards, giving a really good massage, dressing in your hottest clothes and

going dancing, surprise weekend getaways, breakfast in bed, etc. Going out of your way to please through frequent small gestures of reaching out, and doing so on an ongoing and regular basis.

- **Both partners are good relationship "students,"** eager to learn the job better of being the best husband or wife possible. Quite frequently, people behave in a marriage the way they think they should, so they quit listening to feedback, requests, and pleas their partner inevitably offers. In truth, nobody knows how to be the best mate to you. S/he has to be taught what you want and need. Happy couples never quit trying to learn how to be the best possible intimate partner they can be. They're actively trying to give their best, and they're actively attempting to learn what they can do better or how they can improve.

- **Happy couples value their emotional engagement and connection** to each other above all else—even in times of extreme busyness, stress, or personal turmoil. They know that inattention, distance, and withdrawal kill intimacy, so they keep their connection strong, close, and intimate.

- **Happy couples clearly communicate** their desires and needs to each other on a regular basis, so that each knows what matters and is important to the other.

- **Happy couples open up and reveal their feelings to each other.** They share their inner lives, secrets, thoughts, feelings, hopes, wishes, hurts, frustrations, disappointments, yearnings, and fears. They keep their hearts open, allowing for love without defensiveness and protections—love that can actually be experienced.

- **They've learned how to be independent without being distant.**
- **They express their love verbally every day.** Verbalizing love ensures that your feelings don't just stay inside you.
- **Reciprocal give and take.** What I give is moderately equivalent to what I receive. It's two people being responsive to each other. I am responsive to you, and I make what's important to you important to me. We have both adopted the assumption of "us" and "we" rather than "you" and "me," making it a two-way street relationship.
- **Emotional presence.** There is a willingness to share our inner lives with each other, our thoughts, feelings, hopes, hurts, yearnings, and fears. We are nurturing to each other, often best friends, and are generally helpful and compassionate about our partner's struggles. We care about each other's well-being. We have both taken down our walls and have opened up our hearts to each other—and we keep open hearts toward each other, even in the face of our partner's insensitivity, withdrawal, anger, or mistakes.
- **We treat each other well,** with good will, with an absence of malice, and the benefit of doubt. Our positive, kind, supportive, friendly, compassionate comments and behaviors toward each other far outweigh the critical, angry, judgmental, unfriendly comments and behaviors. There is an absence of unwarranted hostility, and we don't regularly dump our negative emotions about other things onto our partner. We both control our anger and reactivity and express those appropriately, knowing that we're not trying to injure love, trust or our partner's happiness.

- **We create time to be alone together and tend to do things with each other.** We make our intimate relationship a top priority in our lives.
- **Stability.** We keep our relationship on solid footing, making sure not to destabilize, threaten, or withdraw from each other. We've learned how to be independent without being distant.
- **We both use good conflict resolution,** problem solving, negotiating, and compromising skills—consistently and regularly.

"For one human being to love another is perhaps the most difficult task that has been entrusted to us, the ultimate task, the work for which all other work is merely preparation." (Rainer Maria Rilke)

NOTES

Pages 9–11. Quiz: How Comfortable Are You in Receiving Love? Reprinted with permission of the authors. *Receiving Love* by Harville Hendrix and Helen LaKelly Hunt (Atria Publishers), 2005.

Pages 21–23. Handling Criticism Better. Used with permission of the author. *I Need Your Love—Is That True?* by Byron Katie (Three Rivers Press), 2006. (www.thework.com).

Pages 24–26. How Do You Disconnect? Used with permission of the author. *The Truth about Love* by Pat Love (Fireside), 2001.

Pages 58–60.What Are Your Hot-Button Issues? Reprinted with permission of the author. *We Love Each Other, But ...* by Ellen Wachtel (St. Martin's Griffin), 2000.

Page 67. A Couple's Exercise to Effectively Resolve Conflict. Reprinted with permission from the author, Harville Hendrix, who used this as a handout in a workshop in Broomfield, Colorado in 2005.

Pages 114–116. The Basics of Romantic Intelligence. Used with permission of the authors. *Romantic Intelligence* by Mary and John Valentis (New Harbinger), 2003.

Pages 124–126. The Way to Lose Your Defensiveness. Reprinted with permission of the authors. *Romantic Intelligence* by Mary and John Valentis (New Harbinger), 2003.

Pages 127–129. Erotic Talk Adds Spice to Your Relationship. Used with permission of the author. *The Fine Art of Erotic Talk* by Bonnie Gabriel (Bantam Books), 1996. (www.lovetalk.org).

Pages 130–132. The Fine Art of Erotic Talk. Used with permission of the author. *The Fine Art of Erotic Talk* by Bonnie Gabriel (Bantam Books), 1996. (www.lovetalk.org).

Pages 136–138. Emotional Viagra. Used with permission of the author. *We Love Each Other But ...* by Ellen Wachtel (St. Martin's Griffin), 2000.

Pages 156–159. Couple's Exercise in Feeling Closer and More Connected. Reprinted with permission of the authors. *365 Questions for Couples* by Michael, Stanis and Seanna Beck (Adams Media Corporation), 1999.

Pages 200–202. Making it Safe to be in a Relationship With You. Used with permission of the authors and from the publishers M Evans and Rowman & Littlefield. *This Is How Love Works* by Steven Carter (M. Evans Publishing), 2002.

Pages 216–219. Quiz: Are You Sabotaging Your Relationship(s)? Reprinted with the permission of the author. *Relationship Saboteurs* by Randi Gunther (New Harbinger), 2010.

Pages 244–246. Forgiveness Requires Letting Go of Resentment. Used with permission of the author. *How Can I Forgive You? The Courage to Forgive, the Freedom Not To* by Janis Abrahms Spring, Ph.D. (www.janisaspring.com) . (Perennial Currents), 2005.

Pages 259–262. Suggestions for a More Romantic Relationship—Part 1. *1001 Ways to Be Romantic*, copyright 2010 by Gregory J. P. Godek. Used with permission from the publisher Sourcebooks (www.sourcebooks.com).

Pages 263–265. Suggestions for a More Romantic Relationship—Part 2. *1001 Ways to Be Romantic*, copyright 2010 by Gregory J. P. Godek. Used with permission from the publisher Sourcebooks (www.sourcebooks.com).

Pages 266–269. Sexual "Secrets" Every Woman Should Know—Part 2. Used with permission of Michele Weiner-Davis (www. divorcebusting.com), *The Sex-Starved Marriage* (Simon & Schuster), 2004.

Pages 275–277.The Cure-All for Disconnection. Used with permission from the authors. *How to Improve Your Marriage without Talking about It*, by Patricia Love (www.patlove.com) and Steven Stosny (www.compassionpower.com). (Broadway Books), 2008.

Pages 278–280. Couple's Communication Exercise. Reprinted with permission of the author. *The Couples Comfort Book* by Jennifer Louden (www.jenniferlouden.com), Harpers San Francisco), 2005.

AFTERWORD

How to Choose a Good Marriage Counselor or Couple's Therapist

There are many counselors and therapists trained to do individual counseling. Some decide to expand their client base by branching off into offering marriage therapy or couple's counseling.

These are not the people you want to choose if you want help with your relationship. You want trained, licensed people who specialize in marriage/couple's therapy—some designation like "Licensed Marriage and Family Therapist" or the equivalent. In other words, you want a relationship specialist, not a psychotherapist, professional counselor, psychologist, psychiatrist, or therapist who specializes in "anxiety, adolescents, depression, and relationships."

But there are so many people claiming to specialize in marriage/relationship counseling—how do you choose the very best one? Here is a guide to help you make a good decision.

First, you want someone experienced—who has done this for a number of years—not someone starting out. (Experienced people tend to cost more than those who are just starting out, but this is one arena in which you are likely to get what you pay for.)

Second, some marriage counselors offer weekly sessions for forty-five to sixty minutes, whereas others work longer (two-to-three-hour appointments), and some offer "intensives" that take several days. Obviously, the longer appointments cost more, but if you can afford them, it has been my experience that they are far more effective. You have sufficient time to deeply delve into conflicts, emotions, or hurts, and then you can create solutions or resolutions in the same session. The goal is to be able to walk out feeling you are really making progress and fixing what's wrong, rather than hoping that you might get this issue solved next time.

As a result, if you work, for instance, in three-hour sessions, you get so much more done, and you don't normally stay in therapy for month after month after month. (Insurance may not cover all of the longer appointments, however, but you hopefully fix or resolve the issues way more quickly.)

Third, look for someone you find easy to talk to. But keep in mind that you are looking for a therapist/guide/teacher/advisor, not a friend.

Forth, you want someone who demonstrates insight regarding the true problems and the dynamics in your relationship. As an example, a couple can enter marriage counseling presenting with poor communication problems, but the actual issue may not be poor communication at all. The real issue may be that the two of you have grown disconnected, and you may be questioning whether you are still loved and valued by the other.

You can see how that may lead to poor communication in a relationship, but the actual issue is the distance and/or the disconnect between the two of you. The therapist who treats the issue as a communication problem is not going to be fixing the larger dynamic, and then you will feel that although you have a great therapist, the therapy isn't working.

Fifth, you want someone who offers you a realistic game plan to resolve or fix what's wrong—and very important—you want this game plan in the very first session. If the therapist cannot articulate an effective and realistic plan of action in the first session, you have the wrong therapist.

Sixth, you are not looking for someone to take your side against your partner/spouse. You are looking for a person who can remain neutral, who can help the two of you resolve the issues between you, and who can lead you back to connection and closeness. (There are some exceptions to this rule—verbal, emotional, or physical abuse; child abuse; or a major betrayal of trust, among others—all of which may require the therapist to set rules or boundaries that fit one person but not the other. Therapists are mandated by law to report to the authorities physical abuse or child abuse.)

Seventh, marriage counselors or couple's therapists that publish quality articles, books or who conduct excellent workshops/speaking engagements are likely to be effective therapists. Obviously, they know their subject material.

Eighth, the gold standard of marriage counselors (including couple's therapists or relationship counselors) is if the therapist can teach the two of you new skills that you can take home and use on your own. The goal is for the two of you to learn how to resolve conflicts or hurt feelings on your own, so you don't need to forever be dependent on a therapist. This will take some time and does not happen quickly, but the counselor who can teach the two of you to resolve your own issues or emotions is worth his or her weight in gold.

Finally, we learn more effectively when we are challenged. Look for someone to challenge you to do what's hard, not easy.

ABOUT THE AUTHOR

Neil Rosenthal is a licensed marriage and family therapist in Denver/Boulder, Colorado. He is the relationship advice columnist for the *Denver Post.* His weekly newspaper column "Relationships" has run in the Milwaukee *Journal-Sentinel,* the *Oregonian* in Portland, the *San Diego Union Tribune,* the *San Jose Mercury News,* the *London* (Ontario) *Free Press,* the Wellington (New Zealand) *Dominion-Post,* and a large variety of other newspapers in the United States, Canada, Australia, and New Zealand.

Regularly interviewed by the media, Rosenthal has appeared as an expert on ABC, NBC, Fox TV, and Radio New Zealand. Neil Rosenthal taught in the continuing education department at the University of Colorado in Boulder for thirteen years and has been a three-time president of the Colorado Association for Humanistic Psychology. He founded the Denver Free University, which became the largest adult education institution in the United

States during the 1970s and '80s. He was also student body president at The University of Denver.

Neil is a former elementary school teacher and lives in the mountains outside Boulder with his lovely bride Roni. He is constantly endeavoring to be a "student husband."

You can contact Neil Rosenthal at:
Phone: (303) 758-8777 or (720) 331-5564.
Email: neil@heartrelationships.com
Website: www.heartrelationships.com

Made in the USA
Lexington, KY
05 July 2018